For JAMES
from Grandma + Papa

Living with a
Border
Collie

Edited by Dita Kilsby

BARRON'S

The Question of Gender
The "he" pronoun is used throughout this book in favor of the rather
impersonal "it," but no gender bias is intended at all.

ACKNOWLEDGMENTS
Many thanks to Judith Gregory (Tonkory); Sue Ader (Passim);
Maggie Peacock (Arnpriors); and Barbara Carpenter (Brocken).

First edition for the United States and Canada published
by Barron's Educational Series, Inc., 2001.

All inquiries should be addressed to:

Barron's Educational Series, Inc.
250 Wireless Boulevard
Hauppauge, New York 11788
http://www.barronseduc.com

Library of Congress Catalog Card No: 00-108148

International Standard Book Number: 0-7641-5326-9

Printed in Singapore

9 8 7 6 5 4 3 2

CONTENTS

1 **INTRODUCING THE BORDER COLLIE**   7
Breed origins; Celtic canines; Developing the "eye;" Coat colors; The Collie family; Early references; The American trail; Early sheepdog trials; Significant dogs; Registries; The breed today.

2 **PUPPY POWER**   15
Finding your pup; Preparing for pup; The homecoming; The first night; Feeding; Exercise; Housebreaking; Family life; Child's play; Resident dog; Feline friends; Early lessons; Socialization; Training.

3 **THE ADOLESCENT BORDER COLLIE**   39
Owner confidence; Submission and dominance; Boredom breakers; Chasing; The Watch command; Catching nipping in the bud; Recall; Humping; Neutering.

4 **THE FAMILY DOG**   47
Exercise; Fun and games; Rescue SOS; Care of the adult dog; Grooming; Veteran care.

5 BROADENING HORIZONS

Good citizens; Obedience;
Flyball; Scent-Hurdling; Agility;
Sheepdog trials; Tracking;
Come dancing; The show world.

61

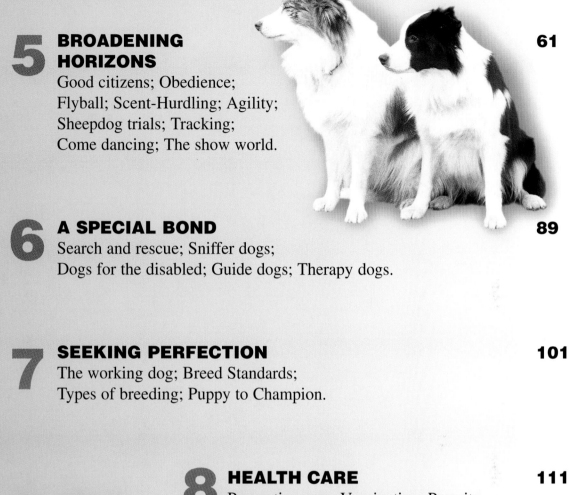

6 A SPECIAL BOND

Search and rescue; Sniffer dogs;
Dogs for the disabled; Guide dogs; Therapy dogs.

89

7 SEEKING PERFECTION

The working dog; Breed Standards;
Types of breeding; Puppy to Champion.

101

8 HEALTH CARE

Preventive care; Vaccination; Parasite
control; Emergency care/first aid; The
A, B, and C of First Aid; Breed-specific
problems; Health summary.

111

CHAPTER ONE

INTRODUCING THE BORDER COLLIE

There is no other breed like the Border Collie. These dogs are supremely intelligent and loyal, and the pleasure of owning a well-trained Collie cannot be surpassed. This is not to say they are suitable for all owners, however. On the contrary, relatively few homes can offer the Border Collie the stimulating environment and decisive leadership the breed so desperately needs. In the wrong home environment a Border Collie can become miserable and destructive, falling prey to a whole host of behavioral problems.

This comes as no surprise when you consider the working tradition of the Border Collie. Bred over hundreds of years to herd and guard sheep, the Collie is a true workaholic and should be kept suitably employed.

BREED ORIGINS

The history of the Border Collie—or Working Sheepdog, as it is also known—is a long one.

Herding is one of the earliest jobs the domestic dog has done for humans. Wild dogs, working in packs, naturally herd their prey to single out one animal for the kill. Years of domestication and selective breeding produced a dog whose shepherding skills could be harnessed for the benefit of man.

In the past, livestock was even more important than it is now—not only to a country's economy, but also to the lives and livelihoods of the individual shepherds; dogs that could guard and herd sheep and cattle (sometimes over long distances) were invaluable. By selectively breeding good herding dogs, certain types evolved, including the Collie.

CELTIC CANINES

It is thought that the Collie's ancestors arrived in Ireland from Europe between the fifth and first centuries B.C. They were brought over by some Celtic tribes that set up home in Ireland,

Herding livestock was one of the first tasks taken on by the domesticated dog.

DEVELOPING THE "EYE"

One of the first things to be developed in the Scottish sheepdog was the "Collie eye." Anyone who has seen a Collie working (or playing) will know the characteristic Collie working position—crouching down, eyes fixed on its "prey." It is similar to the posture adopted by the pointing breeds, and it is thought that Setters, Spaniels, and Pointers could have been bred with Collies to achieve this "eye."

Since shepherds along the English-Scottish border were responsible for considerably fine-tuning the sheepdog, the new type was named the Border Collie.

together with their livestock and shepherding dogs. The fact that the word *collie* is thought to derive from the Celtic and Gaelic word for "useful" shows how important these dogs were to the early shepherds.

One of those tribes moved to the Western Isles of Scotland, followed by Christian monks. If their sheepdogs were invaluable before, they were certainly so now. Ireland's landscape, with its lush pastures, was able to sustain horses and cattle, but it was sheep that were popular in Scotland because they could be kept on that more inhospitable, sparse terrain. Sheep were very important to the country's economy, both for their meat and for their wool, so a good flock dog was invaluable, to herd sheep over long distances, to find strays, and to be a reliable worker in often hostile conditions and surroundings.

The "Collie eye" remains a typical characteristic of the breed, regardless of whether the dog is from working stock.

COAT COLORS

Although you'd imagine that the color of a dog's coat is simply aesthetic, and that it would have little effect on the dog's working ability, early breeders selectively bred certain coat colors for specific purposes. For example, white dogs were often used to guard and herd flocks; black, black and tan, and brindle were often used as drovers; and blue merles were found to blend in well with the rocks and crags of the mountainside, so were used as hill herders.

Despite the early preference for white herders, farmers today do not generally favor them, believing that white dogs are too sheeplike and less likely to be respected by the flock (the shepherds of the early 1900s felt the same way). Of course, there are always exceptions, and there are good examples of white Collies that are more than capable of managing their wards.

Some farmers believe that white Border Collies are not respected by sheep.

NAME GAME

There are a number of origins for the word *collie*. As well as coming from the Gaelic for "useful," *collie* could have come from the Welsh word for "faithful" (*coelius*), or it could have derived from *colley*, a Scottish breed of sheep. It could be even more simple—and have derived from *coalley*, meaning "black."

The name *Border Collie* was given by the International Sheepdog Society (ISDS) to classify this type of dog from the region of its origin on the society's registration documents.

THE COLLIE FAMILY

There are various cousins of the Border Collie, breeds that have been adapted for a specific job or environment. Sharing the Collie name, the Rough Collie, the Smooth Collie, and the Bearded Collie are the most obvious breeds that have descended from the original Collie type. The Shetland Sheepdog is another close relation to the Border Collie, as is the Australian Kelpie that is believed to have descended from black and tan Border Collies exported from Scotland at the beginning of the 19th century.

EARLY REFERENCES

One of the earliest accounts of the working sheepdog was by the much-quoted Dr. John

Caius, physician-in-chief to Queen Elizabeth I, who wrote a treatise on British dogs.

"This dogge, either at the hearing of his master's voyce, or at the wagging and whisteling of his fist, or at his shrill and hoarse hissing, bringeth the wandring weathers and straying sheepe into the self same place where his master's will and wishe is to have them, whereby the shepherd reapeth this benefite, namely, that with little labour and no toyle or moving of his feete he may rule and guide his flock, according to his owne desire, wither to have them go forward, or to stand still, or to drawe backward, or to turn this way or to take that way."

Sadly, Caius does not give any physical description of these sheepdogs, saying only that they are of indifferent size.

A further account is given some two hundred years later, when James Hogg wrote *Duncan Campbell, or The Faithful Dog* in 1790. In it he gives the following account of one of his own working Collies, and its strong "eye."

"Whenever the dog was indoors, his whole occupation was watching and pointing the cat from morning to night. When she flitted from one place to another, so did he in a moment; and then squatting down, he kept his point sedulously till he was either called off or fell asleep."

THE AMERICAN TRAIL

At the end of the American Civil War, wealthy Americans started to herd sheep, and shepherds and dogs were brought over from Scotland to help manage the flocks. Of course, the dogs that were taken with their Scottish handlers were Collies.

When gold was discovered in California in 1849, livestock was needed to provide the miners with a food source. Herding dogs were invaluable for this kind of work. It was said that it would take seven cowboys to herd a thousand cattle, but it took just one experienced shepherd and his dog to move the same number of sheep. Sheep were driven to the miners until the end of the 1850s. Again, the Collie proved his worth.

Around the 1890s, various Scots set up ranches in the western states of America, and once again, they brought proven Collies with them.

ROYAL CONNECTIONS

Queen Victoria was a great fan of the Collie, and her royal seal of approval did much to popularize the breed (in much the same way as the profile of Corgis has been raised considerably thanks to Queen Elizabeth II's love of the breed).

Queen Victoria's dogs were painted by the most celebrated artists of the day. Her black Collie, Gypsie, was even exhibited in a show in 1860.

EARLY SHEEPDOG TRIALS

The first sheepdog trial is thought to have been held at Bala, Wales, in 1873, and was won by a tri-colored Scottish dog called Tweed. Trials gradually grew in popularity, reaching America

One of the early sheepdog trials held at Alexandra Palace.

in 1880, when the first trials were held in Philadelphia. The canine competitors were called Collies and Scotch Collies, and they were tested on their herding and penning ability. Some of the dogs were direct exports from Scotland, including Oscar, a black and tan Collie, reported in a newspaper as having won first prize for penning sheep in a competition at Ayr, Scotland.

It wasn't long before trials became more and more popular in America, spreading from the Midwest in the 1920s, to the eastern states by the 1930s, and the West by the 1940s. By the late 1960s, trials had reached most parts of America.

SIGNIFICANT DOGS

The most famous of all Border Collies is Hemp, also known as Old Hemp. Born in September 1894, and bred by Adam Telfer, who came from Cambo, Northumberland, in the north of England, Hemp started competing at trials when he was a year old, and remained unbeaten throughout his career. He was a fast, agile, calm worker, weighing about 45 lbs. (20.4 kg) and measuring about 21 in. (53.3 cm) at the shoulder. He had a long, straight coat, and was black and white in color.

Requests for him to be used at stud came flooding in once word of the dog's remarkable skill spread. He was a natural sheepdog through and through, and sheep had great respect for him. He was used at stud many times, and he features in the pedigrees of the majority of modern-day quality Border Collies. Requests for his offspring weren't limited to the U.K., and his progeny were sold in America, Europe, and even Australia and New Zealand.

REGISTRIES

The first Collie Club was established in 1881, and it produced a brief Breed Standard detailing the breed's anatomy. It is thought that from this, a new type of Collie emerged for the show ring—the Rough and Smooth Collie, which is longer-legged, and has more of a profuse coat and a longer, more narrow face.

The first official recognition of the Border Collie as its own distinct breed came when the International Sheepdog Society (ISDS) was set up in 1906. In 1950, the organization

THE GREAT ALL-ROUNDER

The working sheepdog.

Fun-loving companion.

Agility star.

Glamorous show dog.

Obedience competitor.

introduced the Stud Books of the breed, compiled from the society's earlier registration documents, which meant that the working sheepdog could now have an official pedigree. British Kennel Club recognition came late for the Border Collie, and it wasn't until 1976 that it was accepted. Since then, the Kennel Club registers dogs as Border Collies provided that they are already registered with the ISDS, or that both parents are KC registered.

In 1940, James Reid was responsible for setting up the North American Sheep Dog Society (NASDS), which all the prominent sheepdog handlers joined. Prior to this date, American Border Collies had to be registered with the International Sheepdog Society in Britain.

There are now several Border Collie registries in the U.S., including the American International Border Collie Registry (AIBCR) and the American Border Collie Association Inc. (ABCA).

THE BREED TODAY

It is the breed's versatility that has made the Border Collie the popular dog it is today. As a sheep or cattle dog; as a search and rescue dog; as an assistance dog helping the blind, deaf, or disabled; as an Obedience competitor; as a show dog; or simply as a devoted pet, a Border Collie excels at anything he puts his mind to.

It isn't just in the U.K. and the U.S. that the Border Collie has its fans. In New Zealand, where the sheep industry is huge business, the Border Collie was recognized by the New Zealand National Kennel Club as early as 1927—nearly 50 years earlier than the Kennel Club of the breed's country of origin!

In Australia, where sheep are again crucial to the economy, the Border Collie is also very popular—not just as a working dog, but as a pet and show dog, too.

From South Africa, Europe, America, and Canada, to Australia, New Zealand, Japan, and the Falkland Isles—people the world over have fallen in love with the Border Collie.

A reliable, hard worker and an incredibly affectionate, loyal pet, the Border Collie really is a breed apart.

CHAPTER TWO

PUPPY POWER

There's nothing more delightful than having a puppy in the house, especially one as fluffy and appealing as a Border Collie. Your home will burst into life—and will be full of smiles and laughter. However, there is a possibility that it will also be full of puddles and teeth marks.

Although puppyhood is a wonderfully happy time, it is far from stress-free. All pups are hard work, but a quick-witted Border Collie seems to be more draining than most, and you will have to spend all your time keeping one step ahead.

Now for the good news. Compared to some breeds, Collies are early maturers. Some types of dog can be seriously destructive and very puppyish up until 18 months of age. Border Collies, by comparison, are quite serious little dogs, and tend to become more manageable considerably earlier (provided you keep up with your training)—so there is light at the end of the tunnel.

FINDING YOUR PUP

Border Collie pups are not hard to come by, but you will still have to do some research to make sure you get the best pup possible. Puppy farms (mills) have exploited the breed's popularity and are producing low-quality, unhealthy pups with poor temperaments.

Border Collies are such sensitive dogs that it is vital you buy a pup that has had the very best start in life. That means ensuring that both parents are excellent examples of the breed, with the best health and temperaments possible. Remember, a new mother can be very protective of her young, so it is wise to see the dam even before she is mated—if the litter is well planned. This will give you a good indication of her temperament. The sire's attitude and behavior should also be impeccable.

Ideally, the puppies should be reared in the home so they will have grown up surrounded by all the smells, noises, and chaos of everyday family life. If the breeder has cats, other dogs,

A beautifully reared litter of puppies with their mother.

and children in the house, all the better, as the pup will grow up knowing how to behave around them. At the very least, he won't be terrified of these "aliens" on encountering them when he is older.

Picking Perfection

The ideal Border Collie pup will be the one that comes forward to investigate you when you view the litter. Be wary of the one at the back that is reluctant to come forward—he could grow up to be a nervous nipper, and is best left to the experienced handler who will know exactly how to improve his confidence.

The puppies should be clean and healthy looking:

- Eyes should be clear and bright, with no discharge present.
- Ears should be clean (and there should be no odor).
- The coat should be in good condition.
- There should be no evidence of fleas.
- The pups should not be thin—you should be able to feel the ribs, without them poking out. The backbone and hip bones should not be prominent.
- The pups' tummies should not feel too rounded or full, as this may indicate the presence of worms.

You should ask the breeder about any health problems in the line (e.g., eyes, hips, hearing etc.), and to see the relevant documentation. Every country has its own health-scoring

The ideal puppy is bold and inquisitive.

A responsible breeder will help you to make your choice, and will be ready to offer help and advice at all times.

systems; your veterinarian or breed club will tell you what certificates you should ask to see. Ask about any inoculations or other treatments the pup would have received by the time you take him home.

Finally, ask the breeder if he would be willing to take the puppy back should there be any problems, and whether he will offer advice throughout the dog's life. If he agrees, make sure you get this in writing. A good breeder will want to be kept informed about how the puppy is getting on, and will be more than willing to be involved. The breeder is responsible for bringing the pup into the world, and that responsibility does not come to an end when the pup is sold. If you have any problems with your Collie, or you are no longer able to look after him, the breeder should offer to take the dog back.

While you're picking the ideal pup, the breeder will be trying to pick the ideal new owner, so be prepared to be interrogated about your working hours, your home, your experience, your family life, your expectations, etc. Do not take offense at such intimate questioning. The breeder has to be absolutely sure that you are suitable for a dog as demanding as a Border Collie.

PREPARING FOR PUP

Once you have passed the stringent breeder test and home visit, you will need to prepare for bringing your puppy home. Ask the breeder for details of the food that the pups are being fed, and stock up. Buy some sturdy puppy toys, some tough chews that won't splinter, a soft, light lead and collar (with a tag engraved with your details), a puppy crate, food and water bowls, and bedding.

Next, you should turn your attention to making your home and yard as safe as possible.

Puppy-Proofing

It's remarkable how much damage a Collie pup can cause. Remove everything from the puppy's reach—ornaments, shoes, plants, etc. Go through every room in the house on your hands and knees, looking for potential trouble spots such as electric cables. Never underestimate your puppy's capabilities. If determined enough, a clever Collie will soon devise ways and means of getting to where he wants to be, whether that is to an open upstairs window, or to devour your poisonous ivy plant on top of the TV. It is better to be safe than sorry, so remove all potential hazards just in case, and always ensure that doors and windows are safely secured.

Of course, there are things that you won't be able to remove, such as furniture. Be warned that puppies investigate everything with their mouths. When you get your Collie home, you should be vigilant and start teaching him the house rules. The moment you see him chewing the sofa, tell him "No" firmly. Puppies are fast

workers. You have to turn your back for only a second and they can be up to no good, so be prepared to have chair legs chewed, door frames gnawed, and carpets ripped up—it's all part of the fun of raising a pup!

Your yard should also be made safe before you bring the pup home. First, it should be fenced securely. Check to be sure there are no holes which a pup can squeeze through, nor any areas where he could burrow underneath. The fence should be at least 6 feet high (1.8 meters) to ensure he can't climb or leap over it when he is a little older.

Some plants are poisonous to dogs, so always supervise him in the yard to make sure he isn't chewing something hazardous. The best option is to have a separate grass area where the dog can play, and where he can't get access to your

HORTICULTURAL HAZARDS

Below is a list of some of the household and yard plants that can be poisonous to dogs. This list is by no means definitive. Ask your local yard center for information on plants before bringing them home.

- Amaryllis
- Azalea
- Cyclamen
- Daffodil
- Dumb cane (dieffenbachia)
- Elderberry
- Foxglove
- Holly
- Hyacinth
- Iris

- Laurel
- Lily of the Valley
- Milkweed
- Mistletoe
- Nightshade
- Oleander
- Philodendron
- Poinsettia
- Primrose
- Ragwort
- Rhododendron
- Spider plant
- Stinging nettle
- Wisteria
- Yew

Check out plants that could be poisonous.

You cannot blame a pup for chewing the "wrong" thing.

It is your job to provide toys specifically for the puppy.

prize begonias. To keep him from digging up your lawn, why not set up an area where your dog can dig to his heart's content?

Finding a Veterinarian

Before you bring your pup home, you should also have registered with a local veterinarian. Finding a good veterinarian is as important as finding a good doctor. He should have a well-equipped practice, excellent veterinary skills, and good interpersonal abilities. In addition to looking after your pet, he should also be looking after you—giving clear explanations in answer to all your questions, and keeping you fully informed about your pet's condition. You will be entrusting your pet's life to the veterinarian's hands, so you must have the utmost confidence and trust in him.

Check your local telephone directory for a listing of veterinarians in your area, and ask friends and relatives whether they could recommend a good veterinarian. If your breeder is local to you, perhaps he could advise you. Make an appointment at the practice so that you can be shown around the facilities and meet the veterinarians. Take a list of questions along with you. What are the opening hours? Are home visits possible? Do they provide hospital facilities? Is there 24-hour supervision of inpatients?

Once you have registered, make an appointment for the day after you bring your puppy home. Your veterinarian will be able to examine the pup thoroughly, and will advise you on worming and vaccination treatments.

THE HOMECOMING

All the preparations have been made, and the long-awaited day arrives at last. Arrange to get the pup in the morning. This will give the

Everything will seem bewildering to the new arrival.

puppy a little time to settle into his new home before he is expected to sleep on his own for the first time (see page 20).

Ask a friend to drive you to the breeder, and take along a couple of towels for the drive home, just in case of accidents. If it is likely to be a long journey, you should take the pup's bowl and some water along, too.

Once all the formalities with the breeder have been taken care of (you have the relevant paperwork and diet sheet, etc.), it's time for the journey home. Put the puppy on your lap, and comfort and reassure him. Remember, this is the first time he has been separated from his mother, breeder, and siblings, and he is likely to be completely overwhelmed by the situation. Plus, he is probably unused to car travel, so don't be alarmed if he becomes a little carsick on the trip.

Your Collie pup will probably be quite tired when he arrives at his new home, though he will also want to investigate it. Introduce him to the room where his crate or bed is, and let him have a sniff around to get his bearings. Let any other family members say a quick "Hello" before taking him out to the yard and then settling him down for a quick nap. Like babies, puppies need lots of sleep, so don't overexcite the newcomer on his first day.

THE FIRST NIGHT

Don't expect very much sleep for the first few nights, since your Collie pup will do his very best to scream the house down! Even though your patience will be stretched to the limits, you must understand that it is perfectly natural for the pup to be upset. This will be the first time he has ever slept on his own, and since he will be in an unfamiliar environment, it is only to be expected that he will be restless.

Get into a routine from the very first night. Give your pup his supper (as laid out in the diet sheet), take him outside to relieve himself, and then take him to his crate. Settle him onto some cozy bedding with a few toys and a chew, pet him and reassure him, say "Good night," and leave. Put some earplugs in, and try to get some sleep yourself.

Whatever you do, do not return to him when he starts howling. It is tempting to give in to his heartrending cries, but you will be setting a dangerous precedent, and the puppy will soon learn that if he wails, you'll come running. A few nights of insomnia is much better than several months' worth, so grit your teeth and put up with the nighttime howling—it will soon stop.

Similarly, if you do not want to share your bed with your dog for the next 15 years, you shouldn't allow him on as a pup. Border Collies have excellent memories and won't forget the privileges they had as a pup, so start as you intend to continue.

FEEDING

Your breeder will have supplied you with a diet sheet, outlining what the pup should have and when. It is important to stick to this diet, at least for the first couple of weeks. Changing homes is stressful enough for a puppy and can cause a tummy upset; to expect his little body to cope with a new diet as well is asking too much.

If, after a couple of weeks, you would like to change his diet, you should do so gradually over the course of several days. Gradually add a little of the new food to each meal, at the same time reducing the amount of his former food, until a total changeover has been completed.

Some foods are too high in protein for Border Collies and will not agree with them. It is advisable to ask the advice of the breeder before changing your puppy's diet, as he may be able to suggest a suitable replacement.

Stick to the diet your puppy is used to while he is settling in.

As your puppy grows, his number of meals can be reduced. When you first get him home, he will probably be on four meals a day. Eventually, this can be cut down to three meals, and finally to two, one in the morning and another in the evening. Your puppy will let you know when it is time to cut down, as he will lose interest in his lunch or supper. When this happens, increase the amount of food given for his other meals. By 12 weeks, some pups won't want their supper, although some Collies still believe they should have three meals when they are seven years old!

PICKY EATERS

If your Collie pup picks at a meal, don't keep encouraging him to eat. Certainly never remove the meal and offer something tastier. To do so would teach your pup that being fussy gets him lots of attention and that if he holds out for long enough, something more appealing will appear.

Of course, if this behavior continues for more than a day, and your puppy looks out of sorts, you should take him to be checked over by a veterinarian.

Some owners gradually cut meals down to just one a day. Some dogs are fine with this arrangement. Others prefer to have their daily food allocation given in two meals. This can be especially useful if your ever-active Collie has trouble keeping weight on.

Uneaten food should always be removed as soon as your pup has finished eating. Leaving it down for him to return to later is not only unhygienic (especially in warm weather), but it will teach your pup that food is on hand 24 hours a day, and he will lose the impetus to dive in at mealtimes. The pup should always have access to fresh water.

Exercise should be limited while the puppy is growing.
Photo courtesy: Karen Dalglish.

EXERCISE

Your Collie pup will seem far more robust than his little frame suggests, but caution should be taken. A puppy doesn't know his limits, and it is your job to keep him from coming to any harm. Before his bones have fully grown, your pup can do considerable damage to himself by overexercising. Exercise periods should be confined to gentle play and lead-walking.

If you have other dogs, it will be difficult to stop your puppy from running around with them, but you should try to exercise the dogs separately for the first few months. Once he is a little stronger, he should enjoy no more than 10 minutes of free running with your other dogs each day. Being so cautious may seem like an overreaction, but a pup can damage his joints by putting too much pressure on them too soon, and there have even been cases of Collie pups breaking their hips simply by colliding with an adult dog during boisterous free running.

Restraint should also be exercised inside the house. Your pup should not be allowed to jump on and off furniture, nor to climb the stairs until he is at least a year old. Look out for other danger spots, too. For example, instead of letting him leap out of the seat, you should carry him into and out of the car.

A pup will get plenty of exercise each day by playing in the yard, and, once he has had his vaccinations, some lead-walking. Vary the walks so your puppy gets the mental stimulation he needs. By the time he is 12 months old, your puppy's body should be able to cope with more strenuous exercise.

Take your puppy out at regular intervals, and he will soon learn to be clean.

HOUSEBREAKING

This is the part most owners dread, but housebreaking is actually a breeze compared with other areas of raising a pup. Every puppy is desperate to be housebroken. Their eagerness to learn is based on survival. In the days of predomestication, dogs had to learn not to soil where they lived and slept—to do so would indicate their whereabouts to predators. Plus, of course, it was unhygienic to soil where they ate. Although we have domesticated the dog, these survival instincts are still very strong, so your Border Collie pup is preprogrammed to soil outside his living space. This is another reason why it is helpful to put your pup in his

crate for short periods when you are not able to supervise him—he is unlikely to have an accident in his own "den" (see page 30).

The key to successful housebreaking is to stick to a fastidious routine. Take the puppy out regularly, and you won't give him an opportunity to have accidents. The following rules should spare your puppy's blushes.

Take him out:

- first thing in the morning
- last thing at night
- immediately after a meal
- immediately after exercise
- immediately after periods of excitement (such as meeting new people)
- whenever you spot the warning signs (sniffing the ground, circling, squatting)
- every two hours during the day

Allocate a spot in the yard where your pup should relieve himself. If you don't want your lawn to be ruined, perhaps choose a paved area, which is easier to clean up. Take your pup to this spot regularly, and tell him to "Busy." To encourage your pup to eliminate on a particular spot, you can use a puppy-training spray (available from pet stores).

Be patient, and don't rush him indoors right away. If he doesn't go after 10 minutes or so, take him inside and watch him carefully. Try again half an hour later.

As soon as he relieves himself, give him lots of praise and reward him with a game in the yard. If it's cold or raining, take an umbrella out with you and put on an extra sweater; whatever you do, don't return indoors right away, or your

Collie will learn to prolong "going" just to enjoy being free in the yard.

Despite your best efforts, there are bound to be times when your pup has the odd accident. You can't ask for miracles right away; just remain patient and stick to your regular regime. Never punish the pup if he has an accident; he won't understand why you are angry, and will simply learn to fear you. Just clean it up thoroughly, and be particularly watchful in case he returns to this spot in the future.

With time, your pup will learn to control his bladder and bowels, and will begin to ask you when he wants to go out. You can then start to take him out less frequently.

FAMILY LIFE

Your Border Collie pup will revel in family life. You will soon become his new flock to watch over. Collies are protective of their family, just as they are of their sheep. I've heard of one Border Collie who has a family of 12 teddy bears. Every night before going to bed, he does a head count, and if one is missing, he'll search it out. Your Collie will do this with your family, too, doing regular rounds of the house to make sure everyone is okay. On walks, he will keep a tally of where everyone is, and will circle around all the members.

You must make sure that your Collie has more respect for you than he would have for some sheep, however, or you may end up being ruled by him. Your pup should learn that he is bottom of the pack, and that even the youngest child is above him in the social hierarchy. Collies are born to serve, and your pup will be more than willing to accept his low position, provided you give him the leadership he craves.

Your leadership shouldn't take the form of bullying or shouting; its key is calm, consistent

EAGER BEAVERS

Border Collies are notorious chewers, particularly during puppyhood, leading some to think they were beavers in a previous life! If you don't provide your Collie with something he can chew, he will start chewing something he shouldn't. Like a baby, puppies need to gnaw, particularly when they are teething because they require something to harden up their gums.

Avoid squeaky toys; a puppy is in danger of chewing through the toy and swallowing the "squeak." Also, Collies can get overexcited and unmanageable at the sound of squeakies.

Give your puppy a safe chew—one that won't splinter into sharp pieces. Tough rubber toys, in which you can place paté or cheese, will keep him amused for hours, and will keep your sofa from being shredded. It will also help to keep your Collie from becoming bored. If denied access to something to chew, some Collies can start chewing their own tails, or racing around in circles. A Collie that is given a stimulating environment and lots of love will never display such desperately sad behavior.

Establish your superior status with firm, consistent handling.

discipline. Lay down your house rules even before bringing the pup home, and stick to them. You don't want the pup to sit on the sofa? Tell him "Down" and remove him every time you catch him on there. You don't want your pup to beg? Ignore him when you are eating and never give him your attention, let alone your food, while you are eating. All family members should stick to the same rules. Otherwise your clever Collie will notice a weak link to exploit, and may become unruly.

CHILD'S PLAY

The relationship between a child and a dog can be very special. However, it must be worked at. They must both be taught to respect each other and to treat each other with the greatest care. Children must be taught that the puppy is not a toy, but a sentient creature that feels pain and hurt.

Teasing the pup should never be tolerated. Border Collies are little elephants that never forget, and are more than capable of bearing a grudge well into adulthood. The moment

A puppy must learn to play gently with children.

your puppy comes into the room, children should be taught to settle down. Puppies are very fragile—if one is dropped, or stepped on, considerable damage can be inflicted.

Inhibiting the Bite

Your puppy should learn that children are fragile, too. All breeds of puppy should be taught to inhibit their bite, but it is particularly important in the Border Collie, who was once bred to nip stubborn sheep. The moment he starts to chew fingers or someone's clothes, he should be stopped immediately.

- Teach your children to squeal in a high-pitched voice, or to say "No!" sharply, the moment the puppy starts mouthing them.
- Puppies make a similar sound if one of their littermates bites them too hard, and so your pup will understand he has overstepped the mark.
- As soon as the child has squealed, he must ignore the pup to signal the end of the game. Puppies hate to be ignored, and your

Collie will soon learn to be more careful next time he plays.

- Of course, it isn't just children who should react this way; everyone the puppy encounters should follow the same course of action so he grows up to learn that mouthing is never tolerated.

Possession Obsession

To prevent your puppy from becoming possessive of his bed, food bowl, or toys, he should learn that, because you and all other human beings are dominant over him, you have the right to touch and take his things. If all the family spends a few minutes every day on the following exercise, it will prevent potential problems from developing.

A few treats dropped in a food bowl will keep a puppy from becoming overpossessive.

- Put your pup's empty food bowl down on the floor.
- When he has dived in and realized there's nothing in it, pick up the bowl and put a small amount of food in.
- Repeat until he's had his allowance.
- Your pup will soon learn to welcome his bowl being touched since it means he will be rewarded with food.

Do the same with your Collie's toys.
- When he is playing with his favorite toy, hold it gently and tell him to "Give."
- Pull it gently (do not force it out of his mouth, or you could hurt his mouth or break his teeth).
- As soon as he relinquishes the toy, praise him, give him a tasty treat, and give the toy right back to him.
- Again, your Collie will learn that it is in his best interests to give you whatever you want, as he will be rewarded handsomely for doing so.

RESIDENT DOG

Introducing your pup to the resident family dog should be handled sensitively. You want to make your home as friendly and welcoming for the pup as possible, but you do not want to put your existing dog's nose out of joint or he will resent the pup. For canine harmony in the home, try the following.

Keep the two of them separate for the first day. Let the pup settle in and find his feet before introducing him to his new doggie friend.

Be tactful when introducing a new puppy to the resident dog.

You should introduce the pup and dog on neutral territory, so your dog doesn't feel he must defend his property. Because your pup won't have had his puppy vaccinations, a local park, which otherwise would make an ideal meeting place, is out of the question. Instead, ask friends if you can borrow their yard (first ensuring that their dogs are fully vaccinated).
- Put the pup in the yard, and then introduce your dog. Make sure they are free—leads can make dogs nervous.
- Ensure there are no toys over which they can argue.
- Let them sniff each other, and call your dog to you frequently. Every time he comes to you, praise and pet him. Show him that he

doesn't need to consider the newcomer a threat.

- Don't overreact if your dog growls a bit to show the pup who's boss. To interfere would exacerbate the problem, and would signal to the pup that he's more important than his canine senior.
- Never leave the pup and dog unsupervised until they have fully accepted each other, and always ensure that the pup is not allowed to pester the dog too much. Pups can be very testing and can tire out an older dog very easily, causing tempers to flare.
- You need to reinforce your dog's superiority over his junior. Always feed the pup after your dog, make the puppy wait for the older dog to go through a door, etc.

FELINE FRIENDS

Border Collies can become firm friends with a family cat, but it may take some hard work to get to this stage. Some Collies take to a cat right away, but others may become absolutely transfixed, believing it is a new toy to be herded day and night!

- When you bring the puppy home, make sure he is kept away from the cat. Keep them in separate rooms until the puppy has settled into his new home. Meeting what could be an irate cat is too much for a little pup to cope with on his first day!
- On the second day, once the pup is feeling more confident, take him to meet the resident cat.

In time, a dog and a cat will learn to be friends.

- Put the cat on your lap, stroking and reassuring her.
- The Border Collie is a very nosy breed, and it won't be long before your pup comes over to investigate.
- Speak reassuringly to both animals and let your Collie sniff the cat, encouraging him to treat the puss "Gently."
- The puppy will already carry your scent, and your cat should recognize him as part of her family. This is not to say that she will welcome the boisterous, unpredictable pup with open paws, however!
- After a short introduction, take the pup away to a secure, puppy-proof part of the house, and give the cat lots of attention to stop any feelings of jealousy.

- Repeat these introductions, and gradually lengthen the time they spend in each other's company, but ensure that they are closely supervised at all times.

If your pup starts herding the cat, you should tell him "No" immediately and divert his attention—throw a ball for him to retrieve, for example. Most cats will refuse to be herded, and will soon put a stop to such behavior with a quick hiss and a swipe. However, you should always make sure your cat has a retiring place, safely out of the dog's reach. The tops of high cupboards are good vantage points, and once your cat realizes she can keep a close eye on the dog without the dog being able to reach her, she will become more confident.

If introducing a cat to an adult dog, the same method of introduction should be employed, but you will have to be especially careful, as your adult will be faster and more difficult to handle than a pup. A well-trained Collie (as yours should be) should not prove difficult because you will be able to control him with the Sit, Down, and Stay commands.

Cats are notorious for bringing home the spoils of their hunt—birds, mice, anything they can lay their paws on. Since worms can be passed on very easily this way, you should not only ensure that your cat receives regular worming treatment, but also that your Collie's worming is always kept up to date—particularly as it is not unheard of for a Collie to steal the cat's hunting trophies. You will also need to maintain a regular flea control program (see Chapter 8).

EARLY LESSONS
Jumping Up

Your Collie should learn from the start that the correct way to greet someone is to sit in front of them, and wait for their attention. The pup's natural reaction is to leap at all and sundry in a frenzy of excitement. Faced with a whirling dervish, bouncing at 10 jumps a second, most people's reaction is to bend down and pet the cute bundle of fluff. By doing so, the visitor has played right into the pup's paws!

To keep visitors from being leapt on by a much heavier adult Collie in the future, you should nip your Collie's bounces in the bud.

- Instruct all visitors to ignore the pup until he is quiet. They shouldn't look at him, talk to him—nothing.

Jumping up is a bad habit and should be nipped in the bud.

- This will initially make your Collie work harder to get your visitors' attention, but he must learn that his attention-seeking efforts will be in vain.
- Ask all visitors to cross their arms and look anywhere but at the pup.
- The moment the pup sits down and is still, he should be instantly rewarded with a cuddle.
- He'll soon understand that the best way of getting attention is to sit quietly and to wait to be approached.

Door Manners

Teach your pup not to rush through doors ahead of you unless he is instructed to do so. This will save you tripping over the dog whenever you bring packages in, and should keep him from racing out of an open door onto a busy road, or other possible dangers.

- Tell your pup to "Sit" and to "Stay" (see pages 35–36) a few feet away from a door.
- Open the door a little, and attempt to walk through.
- If your eager Collie pup attempts to rush ahead of you, stop him with your leg—just bar his access.
- Pick him up, put him back to where he was sitting before, and repeat the exercise.
- When he sits and stays as you walk through, hold open the door and call him to you. Give lots of praise and a treat.

Crates

Crates are great! God's gift to puppy owners. They are cages in which you can put your

A puppy will soon regard his crate as his own special den.

puppy, safe in the knowledge he can't come to any harm. They are useful if you need to leave your pup unsupervised for an hour during the day; they are useful for car travel and housebreaking; they make a cozy bed for the night, allowing you to sleep peacefully, knowing he can't chew any electrical wires or the cat; the list of uses is endless. Many puppies use their crates all their lives, so it is worth investing in one which is large enough for an adult Collie to be able to move around easily.

Crates should never be abused. Your pup should never be confined in his crate for long periods of time, nor should a crate be seen as a puppy prison, somewhere he is put if he has been naughty. Instead, his crate should be his own little den, a place where he can rest undisturbed. With some soft bedding, a chew, and some toys, a crate can be a little haven, somewhere your pup will retire to of his own accord.

- Introduce your Collie to the crate by putting him in it, together with some of his favorite toys and a safe chew.
- Leave the door open and stay with him, encouraging him to play with the toys or to nibble his chew.
- When he seems happy in the crate (it may take a few sessions) and is preoccupied with his toys and chew, close the door for just a couple of minutes.
- Lengthen the amount of time during which the door is closed.

Car Travel

Although your pup may be sick a few times in the car at first, the more he gets used to car travel, the better he will like it. The problem is, Collies often enjoy it *too* much, and you may have to contend with an overexcited howling beast in the back. The following exercises should prevent this.

- Put your puppy in the crate in the back of the car. Give him some toys and a chew to amuse himself.
- After a few sessions, turn the engine on for a short time, then take him out to the yard to play.
- Progress to a short drive around the block, gradually extending the length of the journey.

- Once he is vaccinated, take him to some exciting places so he doesn't think a journey always ends up at the veterinarian's office.
- When he is happy in the car, you should make sure you include some short drives where you go nowhere. Drive around some streets and then return home. This is to keep your Collie from thinking that every time he gets in the car, he will be taken for a walk. This should keep a lid on any excited screaming.

SOCIALIZATION

Border Collie puppies should be socialized to as many new experiences as early as possible. Simply put, socialization means introducing the pup to all that the world can offer so that, when he is older, he can take everything in stride.

The confident puppy will take all new experiences in stride.

Experiencing new things as an adult can be scary for humans, who are able to rationalize; just think how unnerving it can be for an adult dog to encounter, for example, someone wearing a crash helmet. If they have never seen it before, they may think the aliens have landed! A scared dog is an unpredictable dog, who may attack through fear, so it is crucial he is shown as much of the world as is humanly possible.

The trouble is that socialization should ideally take place way before the puppy has had his vaccinations and can safely explore the world with you. There are ways around this.

- Bring the world to you! Ask willing friends and family to visit as much as possible. Young and old, male and female— your Collie should meet as varied a mix of people as possible. If your visitors give your pup a treat and lots of attention, he will soon learn to welcome all human contact.
- Ask someone to walk around the yard carrying an umbrella while you distract your pup with a game.
- Ask someone to push a baby carriage or a wheelchair around the yard.
- Ask someone to wear a hat/motorcycle helmet/sunglasses while meeting your pup.
- Ask someone to skateboard/rollerblade/ cycle past your pup.
- Ask someone to vacuum in the same room as the pup. Again, you should distract him with a treat or a game.
- Put your pup in the car and drive around busy streets, where he will see the world

safely behind glass. He'll hear all the noises (brakes, children screaming, motorcycles, and so on) and will see all the hustle-bustle of everyday life, secure in his own space.

As soon as the pup is protected by his vaccinations and can be taken out to public places, take him for walks along nearby streets, gradually walking to busier and busier areas. Show him a treat in your hand, and break off small pieces along the way to encourage him to see the experience as a rewarding one. Sit in a bus station for a while, take him on a train, take him in an elevator, and through revolving doors. Whatever you encounter on your trip, shy away from none of it.

Throughout all these experiences, you should behave perfectly naturally. When confronted with something new, your Collie will look to you for reassurance. If you act nervously, wondering how he will react, he will take his cue from you, and your attempt at socialization will be counterproductive.

Puppy Play Group

Puppy socialization classes will help enormously with his socialization and personal development, introducing your pup to his own kind. Through these classes (often held by veterinary offices, as well as training clubs) your Collie will learn how to behave toward other dogs and how to read doggie body language. This should keep him from getting into lots of scrapes when he is older.

Your pup will learn many valuable experiences—how to initiate play, when to back off, how to play more gently, etc. Early

When your puppy has completed his vaccinations, he will be able to explore the outside world.

socialization with many other dogs is crucial, even if you have a dog at home. Your puppy will learn to make friends with dogs of all shapes, sizes, and colors, holding him in good stead for when he encounters other dogs in the park, walking along the street, etc.

The downside is that one bad experience can stay with a Collie for the rest of his life. As previously stated, Collies have excellent memories, and the saying "Once bitten, twice shy" could have been written with the breed in mind. There are tales of Collies forever bearing grudges against a particular type of dog as a result of one bad encounter. If handled correctly, however, this needn't be the case. If your Collie is bullied by another pup, you shouldn't immediately run to his rescue. Give them time to sort out their own differences.

If it looks as if this isn't going to happen, ignore your pup and ask the bully's owner to remove their dog. If you make a fuss of your Collie he will pander to it, believing that a scared reaction is a surefire way of getting lots of attention.

TRAINING

Training is essential with a Border Collie. Not only is it important to keep him mentally stimulated, but it is also crucial for your relationship together. A Border Collie respects his trainer, and you will lay the foundations of a firm bond together if you start training while the pup is young.

Before you sign up for training sessions, go to a few classes to see how they operate. Check that the dogs are trained with positive, reward-based methods, rather than by harsh, punitive ones. Is the class well organized? Do the pupils seem happy? Would you be willing for your dog to be taught by the methods used?

The pup is not eligible for training classes until he has had his puppy vaccinations, but you can begin basic training at home. No pup is too young to learn.

Name

Choose a name for your pup as quickly as possible.

- Say the name every time you talk to the puppy.
- Make sure he associates the name with good things—being loved, petted, fed, etc.
- Say his name in a soothing tone of voice.

Sound excited and enthusiastic when you call your puppy.

Recall

This is one of the most important training exercises. You should teach him from an early age *always* to come when called. Fun training based on play is the most successful way of teaching the Recall exercise.

- Kneel just a short distance from your pup and call him to you, saying his name followed by the word "Come!" Be really excited, clapping your hands on your thighs, showing him a toy or a treat, using anything to get him to come to you.
- As soon as he gets to you, give him lots of praise and reward him the treat or toy.
- Move a short distance back and repeat the exercise, always acting as if you are really pleased to see him.

Reward him with a treat or a toy.

- Increase the distance with time, and start hiding out of sight in different rooms in the house. Practice in the yard and, eventually, in a public park.
- Never shout at your pup if he doesn't come to you. Instead, be more energetic and fun to be with.
- Keep really mouthwatering treats in your pocket, and give them randomly to your pup throughout a walk, so that it is always in his best interest to come to you.
- As soon as he comes, hold his collar gently, give him a treat, and send him off to play.

Sit

Do not force your dog into a Sit. The moment you start trying to force a Border Collie to do anything is the moment he will start doing the complete opposite.

There's no need to force your pup to do anything—the secret is to make him *want* to do it.

- Show your puppy a tasty treat (or a toy).
- He will follow the treat/toy with his head and will try to get it.
- Lure him into the Sit position by holding the treat/toy above his nose, so that he has to lean back (and put his bottom on the floor) to reach it.
- As soon as he sits, say "Sit," and give him the treat or toy he has worked so hard for.
- Practice several times a day, and your Collie will soon start sitting on the word command alone.

Hold a treat above the puppy's head, and he will automatically go into the Sit position.

- Phase out the rewards, eventually giving them out randomly. Never withdraw them altogether, or your Collie won't have an incentive for doing as you ask.

Down

The same lure-training principle is used for the Down.

- Put your Collie in the Sit (as above).
- Show him the treat/toy and hold it to the floor, beneath your hand.
- Your Collie will try to get the reward and will probably break his Sit, stooping down to reach it.
- Eventually, he'll realize that the only way to get close enough to it is to drop to the ground.

Lower a treat toward the floor, and your puppy will follow it into the Down.

The Stay needs to be built up in easy stages.

- The moment he does this, say "Down," give him the treat/toy, and praise him!
- Practice frequently until he drops down immediately.

Stay

Keeping an active Border Collie in one place when he is awake is not the easiest thing to achieve. However, if there is one thing the Border Collie enjoys more than racing around, it is serving his owner. As long as you make learning the Stay more fun than rushing around like a lunatic, you have a good chance.

- Put your pup in the Sit position.
- Take a step back, say "Stay" firmly, wait for no more than three seconds, and immediately return to your Collie, giving him lots of praise.
- If he breaks the Stay, just start again.
- When he will reliably stay put for three seconds at one step away, increase the distance gradually, and make him wait for longer before you return to him.

- If he consistently breaks a Stay, take a step closer to him, and shorten the length of the wait.
- Stays are very boring for puppies, so keep training sessions short, and always reward him for his hard work with a lot of love, a treat, and a game.

No

This is a word you will hear a lot in the next few months! "No" is a word that, said in the right way, will stop a pup in his tracks. You should be very stern and sound as if you are very disapproving. As soon as the pup stops whatever mischief he is up to, distract him with a few training exercises—tell him to "Sit," to go "Down," etc. and reward him when he responds.

Collar

To make lead-training easier (see the next page), it is useful if your puppy is already accustomed to wearing a collar.

- Buy the softest, lightest collar you can.
- Put it on your pup, initially keeping it loose.
- Your puppy is likely to try to get out of it, but you should distract him with a fun game or some treats.
- Never leave him unsupervised while he is wearing the loose collar, as it could get caught on something and strangle him.
- Gradually increase the length of time the collar is kept on, and make it tighter. The ideal fit is where you can get two of your fingers underneath it quite easily.

Your Collie pup shouldn't have any qualms about people leaning forward to touch his collar. Such behavior can be quite threatening to dogs, but you should get as many people as possible to lean over your pup, holding his collar with one hand and giving him a treat with the other. Far from fearing the approach of a hand over the head, your Collie will welcome it.

Lead-Training

Puppies naturally follow their owners around, and you should use this to your advantage.

- When your puppy is walking with you, give him lots of praise, and reward him with a treat for being with you.
- Hold a treat out to lure him to walk beside you.
- When he is walking close to you, at the right pace (his head by your knee), say "Close" and praise him.

This will make lead-walking considerably easier. Most puppies panic the first time a lead is put on, but this is generally because they pull away from it, and then panic at the pressure that is applied to their neck. Once you have taught the pup to walk beside you off-lead, put a light collar and lead on him and repeat the exercise. Provided the lead is kept loose, he won't even notice he is attached to it, and so won't feel the need to pull away from it.

Practice lead-walking for short, frequent sessions in your yard; when your pup has had his vaccinations, progress to walking in a public park. When his confidence grows, you can introduce more distractions, until he is happily walking beside you along a busy street.

Use lots of encouragement with lead-training.

CHAPTER THREE

THE ADOLESCENT BORDER COLLIE

Like any breed of dog, the Border Collie undergoes many changes during adolescence—and not all of them are of a physical nature. With hormones suddenly kicking into action, your cute little pup can be transformed into a rebellious teenager. Provided your handling is correct, your Collie's adolescence shouldn't cause too many headaches. Perhaps your dog's Recall will be a little slower, or maybe he will take up humping as a hobby, but most Border Collies do not cause significant problems for their owners. However, if things *do* go wrong, they can go wrong very badly, so it is best to be forewarned to be forearmed.

OWNER CONFIDENCE

The Border Collie breed has very particular needs, which many people cannot fulfill. The ideal Collie owner should be confident without being a bully; enjoy the outdoor life; and have an active lifestyle, wanting to participate in training and canine sports activities with their dog.

The Border Collie is a naturally submissive breed. In the hands of a weak, unconfident handler, however, the correct balance of authority can shift, with the Border Collie exploiting the power vacuum to his full advantage. You should always be in control of your dog, and should never accept bad behavior. The boundaries as to what you find acceptable should be clearly defined, and you should always stick to them.

Make house rules at the very start of taking on a Collie. For example, if you do not want your Border Collie to get on the sofa, then never turn a blind eye to him sneaking on there uninvited. Always make him get off. Allowing him to get away with transgressing your will—even if it is over something as petty as sofa access—could mean your Collie is given license to be disobedient in other ways, too, breaking more rules and generally losing respect for you.

SUBMISSION AND DOMINANCE

As previously stated, Border Collies are naturally submissive; however, they can *learn* to be dominant. If given insufficient mental stimulation and if handled inconsistently, a Collie will soon start dominating the owner.

Some of the signs displayed by a dominant Collie include

- nudging and other attention-seeking measures,
- possessiveness of favorite toys/objects,
- racing through doors ahead of the owner,
- nipping heels.

As before, your Collie must respect you, and to do this, he must know your rules. Of course, first of all, *you* must know the rules, and should implement them religiously.

If you think you have a dominant dog, work on Obedience exercises together to help your Collie to learn to respect you again. Then, next time your Collie refuses to get off the bed, you can switch to "training mode," in which you ask the dog to sit, lie down, and so on. When he obeys these simple exercises, he should also obey the Off command. Similarly, racing ahead of you through doors or up the stairs can be remedied by working on the Wait command.

If, despite your best efforts, your Collie is not responding to you (or, worse, is becoming aggressive), you should not hesitate to consult an animal behaviorist, as this type of problem can quickly escalate if not handled properly.

BOREDOM BREAKERS

Border Collies are energetic dogs both mentally and physically. Their minds are always on the

A dominant dog may become possessive over toys.

Make sure you exert your superiority by telling your Border Collie to "Wait" as you go through doors.

go. If they think they can have some fun running rings around their owners, they will, just to keep themselves amused. As a Collie owner, you must stay one step ahead, and make it clear, firmly but kindly, who's boss. Collies love to serve—it's what they have been bred to do for hundreds of years—and your Border Collie is crying out for leadership.

Training with your dog is one of the best ways of earning his respect and of strengthening your relationship. Enroll in an Obedience class, consider Flyball or Agility, or any other canine sport (see Chapter 5).

Additionally, you should keep your dog on his toes throughout the day:

- Ask him to sit and "Speak" before giving him a meal.
- Ask him to fetch his lead before going for a walk.
- Ask him to roll over or to spin during the commercial break of a television program.

Short, frequent training every day will help to keep him alert and will reinforce the bond between you.

If you have to leave your Collie for a short period, give him some "interactive" toys to keep him amused. Balls, cubes, and rubber toys are available. The dog then has to work out how to extract the treats, by rolling the cube or ball, or licking and chewing the rubber toys. Such toys are very rewarding for dogs, and should prevent your sofa from being chewed to pieces.

If you give your Collie a suitably active life, he won't have the time or energy to think up

Keep your dog's mind occupied with simple, fun exercises. This dog has been taught to stand up on his hind legs on command.

cunning anarchic methods of engaging in a power struggle with you!

CHASING

The chase instinct is very strong in the Border Collie. This would be fine if all Collies lived and worked on farms, but the majority do not. Modern-day urban life offers few opportunities for herding dogs to release these strong instincts, and many a pet Border Collie takes to chasing joggers, rollerbladers, bicycles, and even cars. The danger to others, and to the dog, does not need to be spelled out.

Although a strong chase instinct can be detected at puppyhood, it is not usually evident until adolescence. Before this time, the pup is usually too small to cause any problems—he cannot pull too hard on the lead, and so on. By adolescence, however, you can have a big problem on your hands, and it can be difficult to solve.

Spotting a Chaser

As with most things, prevention is the key. As soon as your puppy is protected by his vaccinations, take him for a walk along a street, ideally somewhere that has a lot of traffic. You will notice if your Collie has a fascination with traffic. He will adopt the sheep-herding position. With head low, and stretched forward, he will crouch down and then attempt to run after the moving item. Do not scold the pup for reacting this way. Instead, go home and do not

The Border Collie has a very strong chase instinct.

walk near busy traffic until the dog is older, and until he has mastered the Watch command.

THE WATCH COMMAND

This is a very useful command that can be used in a range of situations. Initially, teach this exercise in your backyard or home. You can then progress to areas that have more distractions, such as your local park. The following exercise gives the example of traffic-chasing, but it can equally apply to other types of chasing.

- Show your Collie a food treat (one of his favorites), and then hold the treat up to your face, close to your eye.
- When your Collie looks at the treat/you, say "Watch," and praise him. Give him the treat as a reward.
- Practice frequently until your Collie responds 100 percent each time you give the Watch command.
- When you are absolutely confident that you can always get your dog's attention, take him out to a quiet traffic area. When a vehicle approaches, say "Watch." If he watches you in these circumstances, you should lavish praise upon him.
- You can then progress to busier streets, where there are more distractions.

This exercise will help to prevent chasing in many cases. However, there are always die-hard exceptions. If your Collie starts exhibiting the signs of chasing (going down in the herding position, or, worse, actually attempting to chase) you should seek the help of a professional animal

The Watch command is an essential aid in focusing your dog's attention.

behaviorist at once. In the meantime, do not let your Collie off the lead in any public areas.

CATCHING NIPPING IN THE BUD
Nowadays, working Collies should not make contact with sheep, but they were bred to do so in the past. They were taught to nip stubborn sheep to hurry them along, and to persuade them to cooperate. Some Collies will resort to nipping people and may also herd them (running up very close behind someone, as if about to run into them, and suddenly turning off to the left or the right).

As with all areas of dog behavior, it is far preferable to prevent the dog from nipping in the first place than to punish him after the crime has been committed. Good bite inhibition from

an early age is essential (see Chapter 2). Also, you should never play-fight in front of your Collie. Not only will this get him overexcited, but it may also show him that you think rough play is acceptable—and, when teeth are involved, it is not.

Squeaky toys should also be avoided when dealing with a known nipper, as they, too, can agitate your Collie. Remember that a squeak is the sound made by a dog's prey when it is bitten. Encouraging your Collie, who is already prone to nipping, to delight in such a sound will do little to curb his inappropriate biting.

Once established, nipping can become habitual, so you should seek the advice of an animal behaviorist. Never put up with nipping, as it could escalate—especially if the nipping is indicative of a dominance problem. If your Collie progresses to nipping a child on the street, there could be very serious consequences.

RECALL
Collies are very much "people dogs;" they want to be with you. Of course, this is providing that the dog considers sharing your company a rewarding experience. If you give little feedback when he does as you ask, you can then understand why he may be a trifle reluctant to race to your side when called.

The big outdoors offers lots of exciting sights, sounds, and smells, and you will have to compete with all these things to win your dog's attention. Practice the Recall exercises in Chapter 2, and make a conscious decision to be more interesting to your dog. Be excited when he

The outside world is full of distractions, and so you need to work on a strong Recall.

comes to you, give him a treat, heap praise upon him, and give him a cuddle—anything to show how pleased you are that he is obeying you.

You might also consider taking your Collie's meals out on your walks. If you feed him only when he returns to you, he should soon see it as a rewarding experience.

Collies who are severely reluctant about the Recall should not be let off the lead. Instead, practice the Recall exercises in Chapter 2 in a safely confined area (such as your yard or a fenced tennis court). Only when you are absolutely certain that your dog will reliably come when called should you let him off the lead in a public place. Before then, do not put your dog's life at risk. If he were to run onto a main road, or get lost and never come back, you would never be able to forgive yourself.

If you are unable to make progress, consult a professional trainer.

HUMPING

If your Collie takes up humping (simulating sex with cushions, legs, etc.), get him checked by a veterinarian, who will be able to ascertain whether an irritation is the cause. Usually, however, humping is simply the result of newfound testosterone, and boredom. If a dog has considerable companionship and has lots to keep him occupied, humping is not usually an issue.

Laughing at your dog for humping, or even ignoring the inappropriate behavior, will only encourage your dog, so you should stop him at every opportunity and tell him "No!" sternly.

When he has stopped, call him to you, do some Obedience exercises, and perhaps play a game. It is important to do some Obedience exercises before distracting him with toys or treats. Otherwise he will think you are rewarding him for humping!

If a dog attempts to hump another dog, sex is not always the root cause; sometimes the "humper's" dominance is being asserted over the subordinate "humpee," which is why you may see bitches humping.

If the behavior continues, and your vet thinks hormones are responsible, you may consider having your dog neutered.

NEUTERING

Unless you plan to breed or show your Border Collie, you should seriously consider the option of sterilization.

Advantages

Neutering prevents unwanted litters. Border Collie rescue organizations are already overstretched, trying to find homes for unwanted or abandoned Collies—and the world does not need more to cope with. Plus, only the very best Border Collies should be bred from or used at stud. To use anything less could jeopardize the future health and temperament of the breed.

Convenience is another significant factor. When a bitch is in season (approximately every six months) she will have to be kept away from dogs for about three to four weeks, and since she smells irresistible to the opposite sex, this is often easier said than done.

Neutering is a sensible option if you have no plans to breed your Border Collie.

For an entire (uncastrated) male, the scent of a bitch can lead him astray in more ways than one, and many dogs get lost in the search for a bitch in heat. Others escape the safety of their home and yard and end up as traffic accidents, abandoning all road sense in their quest for sexual fulfillment.

The health benefits of neutering offer the greatest incentive. There are advantages for both dogs and bitches, including the reduction of mammary tumors and womb infections in bitches, and the decreased chance of prostate disorders in males.

Disadvantages

The disadvantages of neutering are minimal, so much so that all service dogs (assistance dogs) are neutered.

Obesity is the most quoted disadvantage, but this can easily be controlled by careful attention to your dog's diet. Incontinence can sometimes occur in bitches, but this also happens in older, unspayed bitches and is usually fairly easily controlled. Sometimes there is a change in coat texture, but this is usually of little concern to the pet owner, particularly when balanced against the undoubted health benefits associated with neutering.

Modern techniques and anesthetics have greatly reduced the risks associated with neutering, which today, can be carried out at 12 weeks of age or even earlier. However, some veterinarians prefer to wait until the pup is older. Find out the neutering policy of your veterinary practice and discuss any questions and concerns you may have.

CHAPTER FOUR

THE FAMILY DOG

The Border Collie loves the hustle-bustle of busy family life and all its comings and goings. He particularly enjoys family activities, whether it is a day on the beach, going for a woodland walk, or visiting friends or relatives. Whatever you do, and wherever you go, your Collie will want to be with you. A hectic social life will give your Collie the much-needed variety and stimulation he so desperately wants. Thorough socialization at puppy stage (see Chapter 2) should prepare the adult Border Collie for all that life can throw at him and will ensure he behaves perfectly in all kinds of public situations.

EXERCISE

On average, a Collie needs a minumum of two 20-minute walks a day, preferably longer. However, it is the quality of the exercise that is important. The Collie's mind needs more stimulation than his body, so an interesting 20-minute walk, with things to do and see and new smells to investigate, is preferable to an hour of walking around and around the same dull piece of recreation ground.

- Try different types of exercise—perhaps a swim every two weeks. Collies are accomplished swimmers, and it is a good form of exercise for them, building up muscle without putting pressure on joints. There are some special dog pools, or you could ask if your nearest horse pool will allow your Collie to take a dip.
- Don't stick to the same walk; change it regularly.
- Border Collies have a habit of second-guessing where you will be heading next. Keep your dog on his toes by suddenly changing direction.
- Try some of the following games to spice up his exercise periods.

The well-brought-up Border Collie is an asset to family life.

FUN AND GAMES

Hide-and-Seek

For every mile we walk, a Collie must do eight times that—running ahead to check that the "coast is clear" then running back and circling the group to keep everyone together and to do a head count before running ahead again. If one member of your walking group starts flagging, your Collie will keep a keen eye out to make sure they don't get left behind. Of course, it is second nature to the Collie to search—he has been checking for stray sheep for hundreds of years, and he won't start forgetting his training now.

On a walk, give your Collie a chance to use his search skills to the fullest.

- When he runs a little way ahead, stop and hide behind the nearest tree. Your Collie will almost certainly notice that you are gone, and will retrace his steps, and then follow your scent until he finds you.
- In the unlikely event that he just runs off without realizing you are not following, call him to attract his attention, then remain silent until he finds you.

- Give lots of praise and attention when he does eventually find you.
- Next time, hide somewhere farther from your path, and increase the level of difficulty (maybe arrange for two people to hide) until your Collie really has to use his nose and all his very best search skills to find his family.

Frisbee

The chase instinct is also very strong in the Collie—again, an echo from the breed's herding past. Although you should discourage all forms of chasing in a dog with a high chase instinct (one that tries to chase cars, cyclists, etc.—see Chapter 3), most Collies from a nonworking line can enjoy chasing a ball or Frisbee without it becoming a problem.

Not all Collies take to Frisbee games. To see if yours will enjoy it, roll a tennis ball quickly along the grass. If he shows no interest at all, then he is unlikely to take to Frisbee. If he takes the ball in his mouth, that is promising.

Proceed to throwing the ball. Once your Collie is chasing the flying ball to retrieve it, you should be able to introduce the Frisbee. Do not throw it directly at your Collie, as he may find it intimidating to have something unfamiliar coming his way. Throw it away from him to encourage him to chase after it and to increase his confidence. With practice, your Collie should start trying to catch the Frisbee before it lands. Do not throw the Frisbee in such a way as to encourage your Collie to leap higher and higher, or he could damage his joints.

RESCUE SOS

The Border Collie has one of the biggest rescue problems of any breed. Every year, thousands are abandoned or given to rescue organizations to find new homes. The Collie's popularity has proved to be the breed's downfall, with puppy farms (mills) churning out thousands of pups to fulfill the market for these popular dogs. Inferior, unsound dogs are bought on credit cards, with no home checks being done on the new owners and little information given about the demands of the breed. In such circumstances, it isn't surprising that the dogs often prove too much for their new homes.

Collies are in rescue for numerous reasons, including divorce, owners returning to work, and a dog allergy in the family. The top reason given is, "I bought the puppy and he's too active/destructive/out of control." All Collies need to be kept active, but if someone buys a dog from a puppy farm, they are taking on their own set of problems. "When I tell people that their Collie is going off his head with boredom because he has been plucked straight off a hill farm from working parents, they

are genuinely surprised," says Julia Dickenson, from Border Collie and Sheepdog Rescue in the U.K.

Some adult Collies settle as active pets, some need to work in Agility or Obedience, and the very active ones are only happy doing a "full-time" job—such as sheep work or search and rescue. Each Collie is individually assessed to match it as closely as possible to its new owners.

"Although taking on a rescue dog has its own challenges, surprisingly, it can be a lot less hassle than taking on a puppy," says Julia. "A rescue dog is an 'instant dog,' fully inoculated and ready to enjoy life without the boring puppy bit of waiting for jabs and not being able to walk him for a few months. With an adult rescue, you see exactly what you are getting. Even more rewarding is the dog that is taken to his new home and then fills out. When these dogs come back to visit me, their eyes burn into me and say, 'Look at me now, don't I look great?' It is *the* most rewarding part of rescue work."

CARE OF THE ADULT DOG

Feeding

You would think that a Border Collie would need large amounts of food to provide him with sufficient fuel for his energetic lifestyle. This is not the case. It has been said that a Collie can survive on just a whiff of food! Your dog food manufacturer will advise you on how much food your Collie needs (based on his weight). If in doubt, ask the advice of the breeder or your veterinarian.

FUN AND GAMES

The Border Collie is a working breed, so mental stimulation coupled with plenty of exercise is a must.

GENTLE BEN

When Ann Chesterton and her husband, Bill, decided to home a rescue Border Collie, she had no idea how much her life would be transformed.

"Ben is my second rescue dog; my first was a Collie-cross. I didn't go to the rescue center with a particular breed in mind, and when I got there I was undecided between a Shetland Sheepdog and Ben, a Border Collie. Ben had grabbed my attention as he had looked so endearing with his nose pushed right up to the cage. When they took Ben out to meet us, he clung to my leg. He still does it even now—he isn't being frisky, he just wants to cuddle up as close as he can to you. That was it—I just had to have him!

Ben: a loyal and loving companion.

"After I lost my last dog, we went four years without a pet, as I had returned to working full-time. I started suffering from depression and anxiety, though, and it was decided that I would leave my job, so I decided to get a dog.

"Having Ben has done me so much good; I just can't thank him enough. I've cried on him, and all sorts. It's hard to believe how a dog can change your life so much. He's made such a difference: he's given me confidence for a start.

When I was ill, I had become withdrawn, but having Ben means I have to take him out every day.

"We had very few problems with Ben. The main one was that he didn't like going out in the car. We didn't know his history when we took him on, as he was a stray, but I guess he wasn't used to car travel, and he would refuse to go in a car. When he was coaxed in, he would be very sick. It only lasted for a fortnight, and gentle persuasion and very short car journeys soon cured him. Now he adores the car.

"Because he was just a year old when we took him, Ben was still quite puppyish, and went through a phase of destroying all his toys. He never did any damage to anything else, though.

"Ben's still very playful, and does tend to jump up at you. He's not being naughty, he just craves attention and wants to get close to you. He'll bark sometimes when I'm on the phone, too, as I'm not able to give him my undivided attention.

"I have no regrets about taking on Ben. He's very loyal, extremely loving and playful, and makes a great companion. He's a little treasure."

Another myth is that Collies need a high-protein diet. Pet Border Collies need a diet with just 20 percent protein or less. To give more could result in your Collie literally climbing the walls, and possibly developing behavioral problems from his hyperactivity. If your Collie leads a very energetic lifestyle, he may require a higher protein content, but you should consult your veterinarian first.

There are many types of food on the market—from canned foods and mixers, to dry complete foods. Some people prefer to feed a home-prepared fresh meat diet. It is a matter of personal preference, and if you are at all confused as to what is best for your own Collie, you should ask the advice of the breeder. For many people, complete foods are a godsend; they take the complicated nutritional calculations out of feeding, containing, as they do, all the essential nutrients your dog needs.

Whether you feed one meal a day or two depends on your dog and your personal preference. Many Collies prefer two meals a day, but if that doesn't suit your lifestyle, they usually adapt to one feed. Greedy they may be, but Collies are not usually as utterly food obsessed as, for example, the Labrador and the Golden Retriever, breeds that would curl up and die if they were robbed of one of the highlights of their day.

If your Border Collie loses his appetite, it is usually a sign that something is wrong, such as dental problems. Try tempting him with something tasty but not too rich (such as boiled chicken and rice), and if his appetite still hasn't returned within 24 hours, see your veterinarian.

Obesity

Obesity is dangerous for all breeds of dog, causing and exacerbating heart and joint

Do not make the mistake of feeding a diet that is too high in protein.

problems. With a Border Collie, however, not only is it seriously detrimental to your Collie's health and to his quality of life, but it also looks so dreadful! A Border Collie is an athletic, lithe breed who should move gracefully—waddling just does not suit them!

If your Border Collie is fed correctly and receives sufficient exercise, obesity shouldn't pose a problem. If you give in to begging and give too many fatty training treats, however, the weight can start to pile on. Older Collies are at

PICTURE OF HEALTH
Karen Dalglish

A healthy Collie should be bright-eyed and bushy-tailed. The eyes should be bright and clear. The ears should be erect and mobile. He should have a keen expression, and should be alert and responsive, and he should smile. Yes, a Border Collie will smile when he is happy, fit, and ready to work or play!

The Collie's coat should shine with health and vitality; it should not be dull or have dandruff (though this sometimes happens before the coat is cast). You should see the dog's muscles ripple in his hindquarters and his shoulders when he is on the move. Above all, a healthy Collie should look confident.

particular risk, because of their more sedentary lifestyle. See page 57.

If your Collie is the right weight, you should be able to feel his ribs (though they shouldn't be too prominent). If the ribs are difficult to detect, your Collie is probably overweight, and you should ask your veterinarian for advice on weight loss. Many veterinary offices hold specific diet and weigh-in sessions and can give special advice on how your Collie can lose weight in a healthy way.

GROOMING

General Checks

Not only is grooming important in strengthening your relationship with your Collie, but it also gives you an opportunity to check him thoroughly all over. Examine your dog for any of the following:

- Grass seeds, which look innocuous enough, but can burrow deep into a dog's skin. Once in, their umbrella-type hook system makes it very difficult to remove them. The pads of the feet are particularly prone to grass seeds.
- Evidence of parasites. Even if you can't find any moving little critters, be vigilant for dark specks, which could be flea dirt. See page 118 for information on effective flea control.
- Any unusual lumps or bumps. They could well be benign, but it is better to be safe than sorry, so consult a veterinarian at once. If the lump is malignant, a delay in treatment could cost your dog his life.
- Cuts or scrapes, which should be cleaned thoroughly. If any injuries are severe, or you

Regular brushing will prevent mats forming.

are in any way concerned, seek veterinary advice.

Brushing

The adult Border Collie doesn't need as much intensive grooming as, for example, an Afghan Hound, but he does need his coat attended to at least once a day. A thorough daily brush-through will prevent knots and mats from forming. Ten minutes every day is preferable to a two-hour slog once a week.

A Border Collie will lose his coat twice a year, and it is important to keep up regular grooming during shedding. Sometimes, the new coat can be slow in coming through, and until this time, the coat can appear thin and lackluster. This is quite normal. If it proceeds for any length of time, however, it could indicate a health problem, so seek veterinary advice.

- Using a bristle brush, work through your Collie's coat, brushing all over.
- Lay your Collie on his side to get to all the hard-to-reach places, such as his belly, his chest, and under his arms.
- When all knots and tangles have been removed, brush all over once more, this time against the natural direction of the coat, which will shift loose hairs.
- Comb through to collect the stray hairs.

Trimming

This is essential in order to keep ears, feet, pasterns, and hocks tidy. Certain lines in a Border Collie tend to be more "hairy" than others. To make your job easier, it is necessary to have the correct equipment—a good sharp pair of scissors and thinning scissors.

When checking the ears, use your judgment as to whether he needs attention in that area. Never use scissors to trim unruly head hair; hold the ear firmly but gently between finger and thumb, and pluck a few strands at a time.

Next, turn to the feet. Gently lift your Collie's foot and trim around its shape. You may also need to trim between the pads—but only to the level of the pads. However, some Collies may require the hair to be completely cleaned out if it has grown too thick and has allowed the feet to spread. It may also be necessary to trim the hair on the inside of the pastern to give a "cleaner" outline; usually as far as the stopper pad is sufficient.

The hock is more difficult to trim and the hair here seems to grow at an alarming rate.

A comb can be used to tease out tangles.

Gently and firmly hold the hock and, using your grooming comb, comb the excess hair outward and upward. With your scissors, trim from the foot to the top of the hock, leaving approximately a quarter of an inch (just over half a centimeter) remaining. Finish off by using the trimming scissors to "clean up" the contour without altering the thickness of the hair.

Eyes

Your Collie's eyes should be clear and bright. There shouldn't be any redness or discharge. If you notice anything unusual, consult your veterinarian; it could indicate one of a number of eye diseases to which Collies are prone.

Ears

The ears should be clean and should not smell unpleasant. If they are a little dirty, use a proprietary ear cleaner (available from your veterinarian) to loosen the wax, and then wipe it away with some cotton balls or tissue. Do not poke cotton swabs, or anything similar into the ear, as you could cause damage and/or push the wax farther down the ear canal.

These following signs could indicate an ear infection or the presence of mites:

- There is a strong odor.
- Your Collie persistently scratches at his ears.
- There is a discharge.
- The ears are red.
- There is excessive wax.
- Your Collie keeps shaking his head.

Teeth

If you regularly brush your Collie's teeth, you should prevent problems from occurring later in life. Ten minutes a week is a small price to pay

Regular cleaning will keep teeth and gums healthy.

for expensive, and possibly life-threatening, dental descaling under anesthetic when your Collie is in his teens.

Buy a toothbrush and special doggie toothpaste from your pet shop, and brush each tooth thoroughly. Do not use toothpaste designed for human use. Put the toothbrush by the gum and then brush away from the gum. Regular brushing should prevent tooth decay and limit the incidence of gum disease. And having sparkly, clean teeth not only improves your Collie's quality of life—imagine how groggy *you'd* feel if your teeth hadn't been cleaned for several years—but also banishes foul breath, making your dog all the sweeter to cuddle.

Nails

Check your Collie's nails every week. If he has sufficient exercise on hard surfaces as well as soft, the nails should wear down naturally. If you do not do very much road walking, however, the nails may grow overlong. To prevent splitting and to enable your dog to walk properly, rather than tiptoeing on his nails, trim them with guillotine-type clippers.

A Collie's nail color varies from dog to dog (and is not generally affected by coat color), and can range from solid black to creamy white—sometimes on the same foot. With the creamy-colored nail, it is very easy to spot the "quick" (the blood supply and nerves of the nail), but with a solid black nail, it is almost impossible, and this is where great care should be taken to trim the nail.

Nails may need trimming.

Cutting the nails should not be at all painful to your dog, and if you have accustomed him to having his nails clipped and his feet touched from an early age, the procedure should not be at all traumatic. If you cut too much nail and cut into the quick, it will be incredibly painful for your dog. You can avoid this by shaving a little off the end of the nail at a time, rather than lopping off a huge chunk in one go. You might even like to try a "grinder," an electric/battery-operated disc that spins around and files the dog's nails down gently. If in doubt, ask your veterinarian or a professional groomer to show you how to clip or "grind" your Collie's nails.

Pads and Toes

While you are giving your Collie his daily brush, check his feet thoroughly. Keep an eye out for foreign bodies embedded in the pads and for anything that has lodged between the toes. Even dried mud can cause problems, as it clings to the tufts of hair, then hardens, and consequently rubs away, unnoticed, between the toes. Wash away mud immediately after returning from a walk, or carefully cut the hair between the toes if the mud has dried and refuses to budge.

If your Collie has had a dip in the sea, his feet should be washed thoroughly to remove any abrasive sand and salt water.

VETERAN CARE

Border Collies are healthy, fit dogs and tend to age well, often not showing signs of aging until they are into double figures. The muzzle may become gray with age, but the other effects of aging will vary from dog to dog. Some suffer from stiff joints, particularly in the mornings, some may have failing eyesight, and others may become a little deaf—though selective deafness may also occur.

Greediness may also pose a problem, with many oldies discovering a late talent for scavenging. When your veteran actually needs *less* food, but is eating *more*, obesity can result, putting excess pressure on joints and the heart. Keep a vigilant eye on your Collie, and, as when he was a puppy, leave all food out of reach. Some learn, very late in life, how to open the refrigerator, so you may even have to consider fitting a fridge lock!

Your Collie's character may also change slightly, and many become increasingly stubborn with the advancing years. Intolerance may also surface, and you may find your Collie is, for example, no longer quite so willing to accept being groomed and putting up more resistance.

Some Collies discover a disobedience seen previously only in adolescence and think that the rules no longer apply. If your Collie starts transgressing house rules, you should not make any allowances and should point out that naughty behavior is still unacceptable.

Of course, other allowances should be made. You should let your Collie sleep longer. If he is a little deaf, you should be careful to wake him gently so as not to startle him. His diet may need changing to one lower in protein, and he may eat less. Read the manufacturer's instructions, and if in any doubt, consult your veterinarian.

Your Collie may also need less exercise. There are no hard-and-fast rules, however. Some will still want as much exercise at ten as they enjoyed when they were three; others may need considerably less. Listen to your own Collie. If, one day, he flatly refuses to go out, then don't make him. If he is racing around the house desperate for a good run, give it to him.

Your golden oldie should be checked over by your veterinarian, and you should contact your veterinarian the moment you have any concerns, however small, about your Collie's health.

Be aware of the changing needs of your dog as he gets older.

Saying Goodbye

However long your Border Collie lives, you can bet it will never be long enough, and the day will come when you have to make some difficult decisions. Your main consideration should be your Collie. However hard it will be to say goodbye, it is your responsibility, as your animal's guardian, to know when to call it a day.

Advances in veterinary science mean that many conditions can now be cured or managed, so talk to your veterinarian if you have any concerns about your dog's health. However, this is not to say that you should keep your Collie alive at all costs. Quality of life is far more important than quantity, and you should not hesitate about allowing your Collie to die painlessly and with dignity if all avenues of treatment have been exhausted and your dog is suffering.

Veterinary practices are experienced in handling bereaved owners, and should manage the whole procedure with sensitivity. Some can arrange a home visit, and may also be able to organize the cremation if you so wish. Your practice may also have details of pet bereavement counselors that you can contact if you are finding it particularly hard to cope.

With time, the tears will subside and you will be able to look back with fondness and a smile at the memories you have of your special Border Collie.

GOOD NIGHT, SHEP

Sue Shirley has owned Border Collies for many years, and will never forget her first, Shep.

"We had Shep from when he was a 10-week-old puppy," says Sue. "He was my first Border Collie. We bought him for my daughter, but then she grew up and left home. Shep was more attached to us, so he stayed with us.

"Everybody liked Shep. He was a real character. Even people usually frightened of dogs would end up making friends with him. He gave people confidence. He was very funny with our kitten who would sleep in a shoe box. One day, Shep waited until she was asleep in the box, then tipped her out and tore the box to shreds.

"He also loved the beach, and would jump straight into the sea, chasing seagulls. As he got older, he got more greedy and would actually try to eat the mussels off the rocks!

"When he was 12 years old, he developed a tumor in his shoulder, which was probably the result of an injury he sustained when he was kicked by one of our horses. He was quite stiff and it was causing him pain, so he was put on lots of pain-relieving medication.

"Possibly as a result, his kidneys started failing a few years on. His breath smelt of urine—it was a very strong and distinct smell—and he started lying on his belly with his back legs pressed back behind him. Some

Shep (front) had a new lease of life when Gem joined the family.

dogs do this naturally, but if an older dog that has never done it before starts to lie like this, it can be a sign that he is trying to take the pressure off his kidneys.

"Shep had to be put on to a low-protein diet, and was kept stable for about six months. Then he started to lose a lot of weight, and seemed hardly to weigh more than the cat. When it got to the point where we thought we'd have to put him down, he would start to perk up. I said to him, 'You tell me when it's time.' Shep could read my mind. Every time I would think of euthanasia, he would improve.

"Then one morning, I got up and found that Shep had been sick in the night. He hadn't moved, he just lay there in it. That's when I knew it was time.

"I think getting Gem, my second Border Collie, was a help, and seemed to keep Shep going for longer—he appeared to get a new lease of life when she came along. It was helpful for me, too, to have Gem, as it meant that I had something to come home to when we returned from the veterinarian's surgery having put Shep to sleep.

"Even though that was 10 years ago, it still makes me cry to think of it. But some people can't realize it is cruel to keep a dog going. You hear of humans suffering in pain; at least you can do something about it with an animal. After years of living with Shep, it was the least I could do."

CHAPTER FIVE

BROADENING HORIZONS

GOOD CITIZENS

The Kennel Club and the American Kennel Club have organized programs to encourage people to make their pets well-behaved canine citizens. The programs consist of a variety of tests that assess a dog's behavior in real-life situations, such as meeting other dogs, walking in a well-mannered way on the lead, being handled by a stranger, and so on.

Contact your national kennel club for specific details of the programs that apply to you. Most of the required skills are quite straightforward if you have socialized your Collie thoroughly, and if your dog has mastered the basics in obedience. For a refresher course, see Chapter 2.

Some training clubs teach the syllabi for the Good Citizen programs. Contact your kennel club or breed club for details of any participating clubs in your area.

OBEDIENCE

There is considerable difference between having an obedient dog and having an Obedience dog. Competitive Obedience assesses the dog's training well beyond the basics (e.g., teaching him to sit, lie down, or to come when called). It really puts the dog's training to the test with very challenging exercises, such as the long, out-of-sight Stays for which the dog needs to be confident and have full trust in his owner.

The Border Collie takes to Competitive Obedience as if he were born for it. His flair for it is because of his intelligence, plus his love of hard work and of serving his handler. The dog should have a thorough early grounding in basic Obedience before attempting the more difficult areas. Obedience is very popular, and most towns have training clubs dedicated to teaching it. Ask your national kennel club for details.

Competitive Obedience requires a high degree of precision.

Down-Stay

The Stay exercises require a great deal of confidence, so you should never rush this training. A Down for Obedience is taught differently from ordinary pet Obedience, as the dog should shift backward slightly so that he goes down without creeping forward.

- Hold a toy or a treat (depending on what your dog responds to), show it to your dog, take it to the ground, and then gently push it into your dog's chest.
- With your other hand, put your hand on your dog's shoulder and say "Down."
- As soon as your dog goes down, wait a few seconds, then give him the treat/toy and give lots of praise.
- Gradually build up so he has to stay down longer and longer before receiving his reward.

Once this training is established, and your dog will go down reliably (this can take anything from five minutes to five years!), you can introduce the Stay part of the exercise.

- Put a lead on your Collie and take one or two paces away from him. Make sure the dog is not on your left-hand side when you walk away from him, or he could be tempted to follow (because of his heelwork training).
- Say "Down-stay," and reassure your dog calmly.
- Go back to your dog and immediately praise him.
- Eventually, you will be able to walk around your dog in a complete circle.

TALKING CHINESE WHISPERS

Chris Paris fell in love with the Collie in 1990 when she rescued a Border Collie cross called Sam. It soon led to another love—that of Obedience.

"Sam was a very nervous dog who had been thoroughly ill treated. It took nearly a year to gradually build up the bond between us. To help cement our relationship, I joined a local dog training club, and we progressed through the classes. We were put forward for the novice class in one of 12 heats in a national pet obedience training competition—and won! We went through to the national finals and came fourth. By then, the Obedience bug had really bitten me, and Sam and I had built up such a good rapport; it was lovely to look at a dog that had come from nothing and see what he could now do.

"We went through a few seasons, competing in more shows and progressing all the time. By now, Sam was about five years old, and I decided I wanted a pedigree Border Collie to start training for Obedience. I chose Tamarsh Chinese Whispers (pet name China).

"I started training China when she was eight weeks old. I'd kneel down and play with her, putting a name to everything I did. To teach the basics of heelwork, I'd cuddle her onto my left leg, with me in a kneeling

Tamarsh Chinese Whispers working with Chris Paris.

position, and say "Close," stroking her all the time, and then I would immediately release and play with her. It takes a lot of time and patience, but doing these simple play exercises helps to establish a solid foundation on which to build when the puppy is older.

"Even when the puppy grows up, training should still be fun. I was judging recently, and was very saddened by the harsh treatment meted out to a Collie for breaking a Sit-stay. The reason why a dog breaks a Sit-stay is because of lack of confidence; it's no use making him *less* confident by punishing him. You also get a lot of dogs who just seem to be going through the paces at competition-level Obedience. Some don't seem to have any motivation at all. The first rule everyone should remember is to keep your dog happy, keen, and motivated, and make sure all your training is based on fun and play.

"I've always been a competitive person. Years ago, I had horses and did show-jumping and dressage; Obedience is similar—though on a horse you have more control.

"Although I am competitive, I don't get obsessed about winning, as some people do. Winning's a bonus; first and foremost, my dogs are pets and Obedience is a hobby. Winning is wonderful—an absolute joy—but it isn't the be-all and the end-all."

In advanced competitions, dogs must stay in the Down while their owners are out of sight.

- When you have reached this stage (remember not to rush training!), progress to dropping the lead on the ground and taking a few steps away from your dog.

When your dog is fully confident in the Down-stay, you can progress to being out of sight.

- Put your Collie in a Down-stay in a familiar room in your house.
- Walk out of the room, and return within a matter of seconds. Immediately give your dog a treat (or his toy) and lots of praise.
- Over time, increase the length of time you are able to leave him in an out-of-sight Down-stay.
- Once you have mastered this level, you can introduce distractions—remember, a competition will have lots of other dogs and people to divert his attention, so you should make your Collie totally "bomb-proof." Training in an Obedience class will help to

reproduce some of the situations in which he will be expected to compete.

FLYBALL

Flyball couldn't be more different from Obedience. Whereas Competitive Obedience relies on the dog exercising considerable control and self-restraint, Flyball allows the dog to pull out all the stops and really run like mad!

Flyball is best described as a canine relay race. Two teams of four dogs compete on parallel courses, and the fastest team wins the heat, qualifying for the next round. Each course consists of a long narrow strip (51 feet long), which has four hurdles placed one after the

Flyball—a canine relay race—is fast and furious.

other. The Flyball box is at the end of the course, and the dog must trigger the box, catch the released ball, and carry it back over the hurdles to the finishing line. The next dog can then start.

If a dog incurs any faults (e.g., if he does not leap every hurdle), he must attempt the course again once the other team members have finished their runs.

If you are a competitive person who enjoys working as part of a team, you'll love Flyball. It's simple to learn and is incredibly addictive, so be prepared for the possibility that what started off as a hobby might end up taking over your life. Handlers of the top dogs devote all their spare time to the sport, not only to training but also to traveling around the country to take part in competitions and demonstrations. You have been warned!

Anyone for Tennis?

Since for the dog, the ultimate goal of Flyball is the tennis ball at the end of the course, the dog should care about what he is getting. If not, he will amble up to the box and back in his own good time, without the sense of urgency that makes a successful Flyball dog.

Collies and Working Sheepdogs are generally obsessed with tennis balls, but sometimes they need to be encouraged to develop this infatuation. This may take time. Some dogs, such as the world record breaker (Frog) featured in the case history on page 66, are late starters. Frog was two years old before he would pick up a tennis ball.

The first step is to get your Border Collie obsessed with tennis balls.

- Encourage your Collie's interest by picking up the tennis ball and pretending to throw it. Speak in an excited way, telling your dog to "get the ball," etc.
- Roll a ball past your Collie to encourage him to chase after it. If he picks it up in his mouth, call him to you. As soon as he brings the ball to you, give lots of praise and reward him instantly with a treat, a cuddle, or a game with his favorite toy.
- Progress to throwing the ball for him to catch.
- Don't overdo it—the tennis ball should be a special toy and should be brought out only for your fun games together. At all other times, your Collie should be barred from access to the ball, and should be given other toys to play with instead.

Carol Plumbly has had a wide variety of dogs in her time—Spaniel crosses, the Bull breeds, even a Great Dane cross. She had long ago decided against Collies, thinking they weren't the breed for her, but Frog soon helped change her mind.

"A friend of mine went to view a litter of Working Sheepdogs, as she wanted an Obedience dog. She decided against a little gold and white pup. When I saw him, though, I thought, 'That's the one for me.' The pup, called Frog, had very pale yellow markings, almost creamy-colored and he had a little butterfly nose—half one color, half the other.

"I competed with him in Obedience, and it was there that I met a Flyball organizer, Anton. Frog only ever played at Obedience, he was very fast and too hyperactive. When Anton saw him, he said, 'If ever there was a dog that was born to do Flyball, it is him.' He was right.

"Although Frog never picked up a ball until he was more than two years old, I encouraged him to play with one, teaching him to catch one from different angles. The training paid off—Frog was the first Collie in Britain and Europe to beat the four-second record; he did it in 3.83 seconds.

"I joined the Jets national Flyball team, and we worked really hard, chasing the world team record. I trained Frog every day. He swam to build up his strength and walked on a travelator (like a jogging machine) to build up his stamina. The thing about Flyball is that the dog has to do very quick bursts of speed. Then they have to do it all over again. It's like getting a top athlete to race again immediately after finishing a 100-meter competition. The dogs have to have the stamina to give an equally good performance time and time again.

"Flyball really took over our lives, but we finally achieved our dream. Back in March 1997, the Jets were the first team outside North America to take the world

Frog flies the hurdles.

A confident touch to trigger.

to get the ideal start. I would start Frog 37 feet behind the line. The starting sequence of lights is red, amber, amber, green. I would give Frog the start signal as soon as I saw the red, so that he would begin running by the first amber light. He would then reach the start line at the exact start of the race—perfect timing!

"Start dogs have to be particularly fit, as they have to cope with false starts. Sometimes, the odd competitor tries to tire the other dogs by deliberately doing false starts, but it never worked with Frog, as he was so fit and strong.

"Flyball is all Frog ever wants to do. I take him to work, and my boss can't believe Frog becomes this maniac creature at Flyball, as he is so laid-back the rest of the time. As soon as he sees the rest of the team, it all fizzes up inside him. Suddenly it's "Whoooosh!" and he becomes this mad animal!

"Frog is now eight years old, and has had to have a toe amputated on his front leg, due to a suspect lump. This was a very traumatic time for us both. I wondered if Frog would ever be able to do Flyball again—the sport he loves so much. Eight months after the amputation, he is still flying the lanes—in an incredible 4.10 to 4.20 seconds.

"I have another Sheepdog now, Donkey, who is from the same lines as some of the other Jets team, and I have high hopes for him. I think there's another team out there, just waiting for the right time. Who knows? We may be able to do it all over again!"

record—a team time of 16.75 seconds. Winning the world record (which we held for three-and-a-half months) was the best thing that ever happened to me. Until then, the world record had never left North America.

"Along the way to reaching the world record, we broke ten British and European records, and although we cannot say we hold the world record anymore, we still hold the British and European record three years on (16.75 seconds).

"Frog was the Jets' start dog—the first to run. The thrill of standing on the line, waiting for the starting lights, is amazing—the adrenaline takes over. Luckily, Frog is a dog that feeds off your nerves, and it helps to make him more hyperactive for the race.

"The pressure of running the start dog is intense. It's your responsibility to give the team the best start you can. Everyone in the team has to be so focused and dedicated. With practice and experience, you learn how

SCENTS AND SENSIBILITY

Robert Henshall was introduced to Scent-Hurdling through his British Flyball Association club (Bassett Allsorts), something for which Border Collie Abby and working Sheepdog Monty are eternally grateful.

"Abby and Monty were Flyball-trained. Abby is ball-mad, and loves Flyball, but Monty was never that keen on balls initially. He likes fetching sticks, and so took well to retrieving the dumbbell.

"Eighteen months ago, I started training Abby. Although she is mad for balls, she is also mad for everything else, too—including dumbbells—and on occasions, will jump on the platform and throw all the rejects off the board (much to the annoyance of the platform loader responsible for keeping an orderly arrangement!).

"At that time, a dumbbell was a new object, and training at home involved playing hide-and-seek with it. This progressed to hiding it in a dark room so that she had to rely more on her sense of smell than her sight. We played with the dumbbell so she saw it as something fun that she really wanted to find.

"Club training sessions also involved gradual stages, initially retrieving from the other end of the mat, then off the front of the platform, and then from any position. A blank dumbbell was introduced which was actually fixed to the platform. This meant she could only bring back the correct one (unless she was prepared to retrieve the platform as well—which she did attempt once or twice!). Gradually, more blank dumbbells were introduced. Once Abby had mastered scenting out her own one, dumbbells of other dogs replaced the blanks and full team training began.

"Abby's color is red and she is therefore lead dog for the four-dog team competitions where we have a 100 percent win record. Now, more competitions are asking for just two-dog teams. Abby and Monty were paired together for the first time at the last competition, which they won.

"They love Scent-Hurdling. Abby, in particular, is very focused. As soon as she gets to a competition, she starts barking, wanting to run and to take everyone else's turn, as well.

"When the dogs are running back, their tails are up in the air, and it is obvious how much they are enjoying it. The most important thing is that the dogs are using their noses and their brains Collies and Sheepdogs are always wanting to do something, and Scent-Hurdling is very rewarding.

"The scent training has come in very handy for me, too. One evening, I lost a glove in a dark field, and had no idea where it was. I asked Abby to 'Go fetch' and she did!"

Abby (top) and Monty (above) progressed from Flyball to Scent-Hurdling.

SCENT-HURDLING

Scent-Hurdling is based on a traditional Flyball course, but there is one difference—instead of the Flyball box at the end, there is a platform. This square platform is divided into four triangles, each given a particular color—red, blue, green, and yellow. A matching colored dumbbell is placed on each section.

Each of the four dogs constituting a team is allocated one of these colors, wearing a scarf of the same color to show the spectators and judging officials which dumbbell he should be retrieving. Each dog handler will have placed his dog's colored dumbbell in the correct position, and the dog is expected to find his dumbbell by scent alone, bringing it back over the hurdles to the finishing line.

Each time a dumbbell is taken, a blank (dummy) one is placed in its spot, so each dog has a choice of four. At the start of each race, the platform is rotated in multiples of 45 degrees so the dog cannot learn by memory the position of his dumbbell on the board.

AGILITY

Like many other canine sports, Agility could have been made for the Collie. It is best described as an obstacle course that the competitor must complete within a set time. The fastest competitor wins. Faults (such as knocking a jump or missing a contact point) incur a penalty. Standards are so high that, generally, the winner of a class is the dog that completes the fastest clear round.

The main appeal of Agility is that it is such good fun, offers the much-needed mental stimulation so vital for Collies, and lets the dogs really let their hair down racing around. It's good exercise for the handlers, too!

The course consists of various obstacles:

- jumps (hurdles, long/broad jump, the tire)
- contact equipment (dog walk, A-frame, seesaw)
- tunnel (rigid tunnel, collapsible tunnel)
- pause table (where the dog must leap onto a table and wait until he is instructed to jump off and continue with the course)

The agile Border Collie weaves with ease.

- weaves (6 to 12 poles set up in a straight line, which the dog must "weave" through)

If you want to try Agility, why not join your local Agility training club? Contact your national kennel club for details.

Jumps

The height of the hurdles will depend on the height of the dog and your national kennel club's rules and regulations. As a rough guide, the hurdle height for a Border Collie is in the region of 2 feet 6 inches (762 mm).

- Put your Collie on a lead, and have him sit on one side of a very low jump (just a few inches off the ground).
- Ask your Collie to stay, and then walk over the jump.
- Turn and call your Collie to you. Show him a toy to encourage him over the hurdle.
- Being connected to the lead should discourage your Collie from going around the jump rather than over it.
- Just as he goes over the jump, say "Go on," or "Over," or any other command word you wish to use. Once you've chosen your command, be consistent—don't change it, or your dog will get confused.
- When your dog reaches you, give lots of praise, and give him the toy to play with as a reward.
- Gradually extend the height of the jump as your dog improves, but do so only when your dog is old enough to cope with the exertion (see page 73).

- When your Collie understands exactly what is required of him, you can remove the lead.

When your Collie has mastered the individual hurdles, you can progress to teaching them in succession.

- Sit your dog on one side of a single jump, and stand next to him.
- Show him his toy, throw it over the jump, and command "Over."
- When he jumps over the jump to get the toy, have a game with it to reward him.
- Once he has mastered this, and realizes he is to jump over in pursuit of the toy, set up two hurdles, one after the other.
- Sit your dog behind the first jump, throw the toy over both hurdles, and tell him "Over." Praise and reward every time he behaves as you want him to.
- Use the same method over three, four, and finally five hurdles.

Dog Walk

The dog walk is simple to teach and involves walking up a fairly narrow plank, making sure to touch the marked "contact area" at the start. The dog should then move along the top horizontal plank and down the other side, again touching another contact area.

- Put your Collie on a lead, and walk beside him.
- As you approach the dog walk, encourage him to walk on to it, saying "Walk."
- Stop when he stands on the contact area, and then, after a moment's pause, continue

As the dog becomes more confident, he will build up speed over the dog walk.

along the obstacle. Do the same when you reach the contact area at the end. (Some people teach the dog to pause only on the last contact, as most dogs touch the first one automatically when getting on the walk).

- Take it very steadily until he is confident on the walk, and reassure your dog all the way along.
- Slowly build up his speed with regular practice. However, make sure that speed does not compromise accuracy—or safety; always make sure he touches the marked contact.

- Give lots of praise and a quick game with his toy when he completes the obstacle.

Seesaw (Teeter)

The seesaw is self-explanatory—it is just like a child's seesaw (except it doesn't have any seats). The dog has to walk up the seesaw, negotiate the pivot point, and then walk down the other side. There are contact points at the start and at the end.

Because the seesaw moves as the dog walks along it, this piece of equipment should be attempted only once the dog is confident on the dog walk (see above). You will need a helping hand from an assistant when introducing your Collie to this obstacle.

- Put your Collie on a lead and approach the seesaw.
- Encourage him to walk onto it, and stop him on the contact point for a moment (as with the dog walk, some prefer to teach only the last contact point).
- Slowly continue up the obstacle and reassure your dog all the time.

MAKING CONTACT

The dog walk, A-frame, and seesaw have marked areas ("contact points") at the beginning and end of the obstacle that the dog must touch. As well as being there to test the dog's accuracy under speed, the contact points also exist to safeguard the dog's well-being. Leaping too early from the A-frame, in his rush to get on to the next piece on the course, would cause considerable injury to a canine competitor, so it is crucial that your Collie is taught from the very beginning never to miss his contacts.

In the early days, actually stop your dog for a few seconds when he stands on a contact point. As he speeds up, he will still be programmed always to touch the contacts.

The point of contact on the seesaw.

- As your Collie reaches a certain point, the seesaw will tip; your helper should control this by holding the seesaw plank and letting it down slowly and gently.
- When the seesaw has tipped, walk your dog forward, down the seesaw, making sure to stop him on the final contact area before walking off.
- Give your Collie lots of praise and a cuddle at the end, and have a game with his toy. You want to show your dog that the seesaw always ends in fun, fun, fun!

Tunnel (Chute)

There are two types of tunnel: the rigid tunnel (which is like a bendable, large plastic pipe), and the collapsible canvas tunnel, which the dog must push himself through. For the novice, the rigid tunnel is the best place to start, as it will build up your dog's confidence before he has to run blind into the collapsible one.

- Scrunch up the tunnel to make it as short as it can be.
- Put your Collie on the lead and ask him to Sit and to Wait by the opening of the tunnel.
- Hold the end of the lead and crawl through the tunnel (if you are small enough!). Alternatively, pass the lead through to the other side and walk around to the end of the tunnel to take hold of it.
- Look through the short tunnel and call your dog to you in an excited way, showing him his favorite toy.

Start off by training with a rigid tunnel.

- As he comes through the tunnel, say "Tunnel."
- Give lots of praise and have a quick game when he reaches you.
- Your dog will soon understand what is required, and after a few tries, you can stop crawling through the tunnel—simply put him in a Wait at one end of the tunnel, then walk to the other end to call him through. Eventually, you can dispense even with this, and can just instruct "Tunnel."
- As your Collie improves, extend the length of the tunnel until it is at its full length.
- When your Collie has mastered this, put a slight bend in the tunnel, which should be made more pronounced as your dog masters each level of difficulty. Although your dog won't be able to see you at the other side of the tunnel, the practice you have put in will

Progress to the collapsible tunnel.

SAFETY FIRST

Early training is useful if you want to do well in Agility, but be sensible. Your Border Collie should not be expected to do anything strenuous until his bones and joints are fully formed. High (or long) jumps, the pause table, the weaving poles, and the A-frame should not be attempted until your dog is at least six months old, with some competitors preferring to wait until the dog is a year old. With the dog walk, seesaw, and A-frame, make sure the dog is fully supervised so that he can't jump off these obstacles prematurely.

You can, however, train the principles of these pieces of equipment while the dog is still young. For example, the hurdles can be taught, with the "jump" on the floor so that the dog just has to walk over it. The A-frame can be laid flat so that your Collie simply has to walk over a completely horizontal board on the ground. Once the principles and the commands have been taught, you can then progress to increasing the jumps/A-frame gradually, once it is safe for your dog to attempt them.

Speed can also be worked on once your dog's bones are strong enough to cope with the exertion.

JUMPING FOR JOY

Jackie Bromwich has owned Border Collies for nearly 25 years. Previously involved in Competitive Obedience, Jackie saw one of the first Agility displays in the U.K. in the early 1980s, and decided to give it a try. Twenty years later, she is still enjoying the sport, and is currently training and competing with six of her Collies.

"Agility is fast and fun," says Jackie. "A lot of play is involved, so dogs soon get hooked on it. I have to drive over a cattle grid to get to my Agility club, and as soon as my Collies feel the bumps of the grid, they perk up and start whining with excitement.

"I start nurturing an interest when the dog is still a pup. I develop their interest in play, and encourage them to chase a ball and to play tug gently. Once a dog is older and is ready for more formal training, he will work harder on the course to get his special toy. For example, a dog can jump five successive jumps quite happily if you ask him, but if you want him to jump them quickly, you need to give him a reason— and if there is a toy at the end of the jumps, that is usually sufficient motivation.

"Although the dog will start doing the obstacles to earn his favorite toy, eventually the course becomes self-rewarding, and the dog just enjoys doing Agility for its own sake.

Jackie Bromwich with Shona, her top Agility dog.

"At Advanced level Agility, speed is crucial— in the top competitions there can be a difference of just one-hundredth of a second between the first and tenth place. You have to make sure your Collie is completely confident on the course. If you ever chastise your dog for doing something wrong, particularly as most mistakes are due to handler error, you will introduce some doubt in your dog's head, and he may become slightly apprehensive—and apprehension costs time. Praise your dog all the time, and keep practicing weak areas until they become second nature to your Collie, to improve his confidence and speed.

"Collies are great to train, as they are so keen and have such drive—they are quite obsessive about things, really. They have been bred for so many generations to work, and are highly reactive dogs. If they are not mentally stimulated and given an outlet for their energy, all sorts of behavioral problems can develop.

"I have two highlights of my Agility career. One was when Dash beat 300–400 dogs to win a competition final. He was fantastic that day and worked his little socks off to set a standard no one else could beat. The second was when Shona won the first advanced class she competed in, after qualifying to work at this level. Shona was probably the best Agility dog I've ever had.

"I've had my fair share of disasters, though. The most embarrassing moment was when Peggy, who was never the keenest dog in the world, had to do five jumps which were at the edge of the ring. I had a friend and my mother sitting in the second row of chairs by the ring, watching the competition. Peggy leapt the five jumps, then leapt over a row of Boy Scouts sitting in the front row and landed on her grandma's lap. She licked her all over as if to say, "Hi, it's me: Peggy!"

"Agility is so fast, there is no room for error. If you make a mistake, it's just one of those things. You win sometimes and you make mistakes sometimes.

"Taking part is tremendous fun and the dogs really enjoy it. The people at the shows are nice, too. It's different to breed shows where judging can be so subjective. With Agility, a fault is a fault, there's nothing subjective about it. Because of this, I think there's very little backbiting. Agility is a good fun day out for you and the dogs."

have built up his confidence so that he will run into the darkness safe in the knowledge that you will be at the other end of it.

- Speed comes with confidence and practice.

SHEEPDOG TRIALS

There's nothing more rewarding than working sheep with a well-trained Collie. It's what the breed has been bred to do for many generations, and there is something magical about seeing Collies in action. Many Border Collies are still used on farms, but an increasing number are also being worked by hobbyists for competitive Sheepdog Trials. Collies love it, and it is good fun for the handler, too, although a lot of hard work and patience is involved in the training.

In top-level competition, hobbyists can be disadvantaged in a number of ways. Unless they buy their own fields and flocks, they may have difficulty getting regular access to sheep for their training. Also, they may lack the experience of being able to understand sheep and to anticipate how they will react. Farmers working day in and

day out with sheep over a number of years are as clever at reading their sheep as they are at reading their dogs, and this proves invaluable in competitions.

Many hobbyists are not bothered about winning the top awards, however, and just enjoy the training that is involved. If you have the time to dedicate to this pastime, however, there's no reason why you cannot be as successful as the full-time farmers, and you could join the growing throng of very successful hobbyists.

If you are interested in finding out more, there are often sheepdog training courses that you can attend to give you a taste of what is involved. Ask your Sheepdog registry (or national kennel club) for details. Whatever you do—*don't* just let your Collie off loose around sheep. Scaring sheep is a serious offense, and could result in your dog being destroyed. Collies should be introduced to sheep under controlled conditions, and under the supervision of an experienced handler.

What Is a Trial?

In the U.K., a Trial is generally judged out of 100 points, with a certain number of points allocated to various parts of the course. The course should be completed within a set time. Although Trials vary, the basic structure is as follows:

1) **The Outrun** (where the dog at the bottom of the field has to run out and gather the sheep that are released at the top of the field).

2) **The Lift** (where the dog should quietly walk forward, moving the sheep in a straight line toward the handler).

3) **The Fetch** (where the dog should bring the sheep down the field to the handler in a straight line and through a set of obstacles such as gates).

4) **The Drive** (where the dog should drive the sheep away from the handler in a straight line to another set of gates).

5) **Crossdrive** (after driving the sheep through the obstacle, the dog should perform a tight turn to start the crossdrive. At the end of the crossdrive there is a third obstacle through which the sheep should be driven, then turned tightly once again. The final leg of the drive is then performed as the dog brings the sheep to the pen—hence having driven them in a triangular pattern).

6) **The Pen** (where the dog—with the help of the handler—should put the sheep into the pen).

7) **The Shed or Single** (where, after bringing the sheep from the pen, the dog should shed off, from the others, two or more sheep, or single off just one sheep).

Shedding involves splitting a herd of sheep.

In the U.S. there are various levels of tests: the beginner levels are the Herding Test (HT) and Pretrial Test (PT) in which the dog must show controlled movement of the stock (either sheep, cows, or ducks).

There are also three advanced trial courses:

- Course A demonstrates the versatility of an all-around ranch or farm dog.
- Course B requires the dog to show an ability to control and move stock in a very large, open field.
- Course C (sheep only) requires the dog to "tend" to the sheep—to accompany the flock from their pen, up roads and over

ALL SHEEP ARE NOT THE SAME!

As you get more experienced, you will realize that different breeds of sheep will need to be handled differently. Hill sheep can be more flighty, whereas lowland sheep tend to be heavier, and need more pushing. Your dog should be able to adapt to the type of herding that is necessary under various circumstances.

bridges, to various grazing areas for the day, and then return safely home with the flock.

As in the U.K. the number of sheep is minimal (three to five) for both the A and B courses. Course C, however, has 20 or more sheep.

Getting Started

There are no hard-and-fast rules about when to start training a Collie puppy. Some may be ready at six months, some later. You can start only when the puppy shows an interest in the sheep. The first part of training will involve introducing the Collie to a small group of calm, quiet sheep that are used to dogs.

If you want to take up herding as a serious hobby, a pet Collie may not be quite the best dog for the job. Although the majority of Collies instinctively herd, those from working lines will have a stronger instinct for what is required. To do well in Trials, you may need to acquire a pup from working parents, one that is registered with your country's national sheepdog registry.

Balancing

Once a young Collie with working instinct settles into his training, he will run around the sheep and "hold" them to the handler. He will stand directly opposite the handler, on the other side of the flock. If the handler moves to the left, the dog should move to his own left so that the flock is "balanced" between the dog and handler.

Because Collies are preprogrammed to balance the herd to the handler, teaching a Collie to

Border Collies can be trained to herd geese.

A DIFFERENT FLOCK

Your options aren't limited to sheep— Collies can also herd ducks and geese. Because these birds move more slowly than sheep, they can be useful when first training your dog. The beginner levels of the AKC herding competitions (the Herding Test and Pretrial Test) can include duckherding.

"drive" the sheep away from the handler can be quite difficult, as initially, it feels unnatural for the dog. A dog is trained to drive once he has a firm grasp of the handler's directional commands.

Directional Commands

Teaching the dog to herd clockwise and counterclockwise is very straightforward. Once the dog is herding of his own accord, the

The Working Sheepdog must listen to directional commands.

handler will introduce a verbal command. If the dog moves clockwise, the handler will call "Come bye," and if the dog moves counterclockwise, will call "Away here," or whatever commands the handler prefers. Eventually, the dog will understand what each command means, and will follow any instructions given.

Obviously, in a large field, it is not always possible for a dog to hear verbal commands easily, so a whistle is introduced once the dog has mastered the verbal commands. This is taught by giving a verbal command and then

WATCHING FLOCKS

Elaine Hill grew up with Working Sheepdogs, and her father, John Chapman, not only worked his dogs on his farm, but also trained and competed with them. Surrounded by working Collies, it seemed only natural that Elaine would follow in the family footsteps.

"When I was aged 10 or 11, I started working with my father's dogs, but at the time, there weren't many women competing. It wasn't until I was in my thirties that I decided I wanted to try it again properly. At the time, my father had Tweed, a dog I used to work at home, and I persuaded him to let me borrow Tweed for a Trial.

"The first one we did (in January 1991), we won third place in the Novice Class. Tweed was a really good dog, and when you're a novice, you're a little slow giving commands. You're not always standing in the right place when penning the sheep, for example. Although it all comes together eventually, it's good to have a confident dog that knows what he's doing!

"Once you're more experienced, it can be just as rewarding to work a young dog. At the start of the season, he may not be working too well, but if you keep up training on his particular areas of weakness, you soon start to see improvements, and it's nice to bring them on—it's very satisfying.

"When you first start off, getting prizes is very important—it's a visible symbol of how you are doing. When you've been competing a few years, though, you realize that prizes aren't the be-all and end-all. It's the dog's progress that counts. If you work your dogs as well as compete with them, the training never goes to waste, as you are improving your farm dogs. A higher standard is needed for competitions—the dogs should be more polished—but you should still allow your Collie to use his initiative. Some people go too far and end up with little robots. But you want your dog to enjoy what he is doing, and you should work together.

"My first Trial with Tweed was the most memorable. I was so terrified; my hand was shaking like a leaf, and I could hardly hold my whistle. You think sheepdog work is relaxing—which it is when you are on a hill, on your own farm, doing it in your own time. In a Trial situation, though, with everyone watching, it is truly nerve-wracking.

"I also do demonstrations at fairs and other events, and although they are also in front of the public, the pressure isn't nearly as bad—in fact, if something goes wrong, the public generally loves it! In a Trial, it's up to you. If you have a good dog, the pressure is on you alone to give the right commands at the right time.

"Since Tweed, my Collies have all been bitches. The first dog you breed and train yourself is very special. There's a real sense of achievement and satisfaction when you do well. So much time and patience is involved, that it's nice to see rewards.

"Holly is my current dog, and she has had great success. Last winter, she had eight wins and was one of the top nursery dogs in the north of England. When I go to a Trial, I have total confidence in her, and it's nice to have that relationship with your dog. She trusts you, and you trust her."

Elaine Hill with her group of working dogs.

It was the breeder of Marie Jordan's two Border Collies who got her involved in Working Trials and Tracking. Having already trained her Collies in Obedience, and having been a regular exhibitor at the show ring, Marie decided to add another hobby to her dogs' list of achievements.

"I start training the dogs to search for things when they are about eight weeks old," says Marie. "It involves a lot of play—hiding the puppy's toy behind something for him to 'hunt' it out, for example. As soon as the pup has found the toy, reward him with a good play. Some people give tidbits; some use a combination of both play and treats.

"It's also important to introduce the pup to different textures. Most Working Trials/Tracking people have their new pups playing with almost anything: metal, plastic, leather, cloth, etc., as long as it is safe for the puppy. That way, he will grow up willing to pick up anything (and, sometimes on a walk, everything!). Some people train their pups to find spark plugs and all sorts of things. Of course, to the dog, a toy's a toy; he doesn't care what he is looking for. Caution should be exercised, though, as the pup shouldn't be expected to hold any articles until his adult teeth are through and he has finished teething.

"I start with simple little puppy tracks at 12 weeks, where the dog has to follow a very short, straight line, with his favorite toy at the end for his reward, and progress from there.

"I've already had some success. Skew (Laetare Music's Coda From Jakovall CDex, UDex) has a few titles to his name, and I've just started working his younger full-sister Fynn (Laetare Cerafyn For Marie At Jakovall JW).

"My dogs and I get a lot of enjoyment from Tracking and Trials. At the last trial, Skew pulled me over in the excitement of following the track. Basically, it is great fun. Unlike Obedience, you are telling your dog what to do and where to go. He is responding, and you are working in partnership with your dog.

"As a handler, you have to learn to trust your dog's instincts, too. It's great fun to stand in the middle of a field, put the harness and the line on your dog, tell him to 'Track on,' and not have a clue where you should be going. Then your dog puts his head down, puts his nose to the ground, and starts following the track. When you get to the end, having found all the articles, there is a great sense of achievement."

Skew (Laetare Music's Coda From Jakovall CDex, UDex) setting off on the track from the start pole.

giving the whistle equivalent. With time, the whistle signal alone can be used.

The principles sound simple, but training a reliable sheepdog involves considerable time and patience, and many hours of working outdoors in all types of conditions. Once you've cracked it, though, it must be one of the most rewarding and absorbing activities there is.

TRACKING

Tracking is a very challenging but rewarding sport, which relies on a dog being able to

ON THE RIGHT TRACK

In the U.K., tracking is part of the Working Trials syllabus, but in the U.S., it is a sport in its own right.

recognize and follow human scent along a track. The length and age of the track, and the number of turns it contains, vary according to the level of difficulty attempted.

Although Border Collies are not scenthounds, they are very good at using their noses. You only have to see one sniffing out a lost sheep to realize that they can offer stiff competition on a track.

COME DANCING

Dancing with your dog is a fast-growing sport that has two distinctive styles. Deriving from Obedience Heelwork exercises, **Heelwork to Music** is very precise, with intricate footsteps and dance steps. Your dog can't be more than four feet away, so Heelwork to Music involves no distance work (where the dog works away from you). It provides a good grounding for people interested in progressing to the more elaborate routines of **Musical Freestyle**, where anything goes. In Musical Freestyle, the routines are more showy, with dogs leaping, spinning, and weaving, and the emphasis is more on the artistic element than merely on precision.

Neither style is officially recognized by the Kennel Club or the American Kennel Club, but there are thriving training clubs and organizations that organize their own competitions. One such body is the World Canine Freestyle Organization in Brooklyn, New York, which has devised its own titles for both Heelwork to Music and Musical Freestyle, awarding bronze, silver, and gold awards according to the level of proficiency achieved.

Most routines are performed in a ring measuring about 35 by 70 feet, and last between 90 seconds and 3 minutes. Because presentation is so important to the routine's overall impression, costumes are a very important feature, particularly in Freestyle. Some performers wear the most amazing and glamorous outfits, and their dogs often sport matching garb.

Being lithe and agile, Border Collies are well suited to Freestyle. They move elegantly and gracefully, and are a joy to watch. It also satisfies the Collie thirst for learning, and allows you to share quality—but fun—training time together.

Try the exercises below if you think you'd like to try Freestyle. Once you've practiced,

FANCY FOOTWORK

Patie Ventre is the founder of the World Canine Freestyle Organization, based in Brooklyn, New York. Previously she was responsible for bringing Freestyle teams together for demonstrations and competitions. On one occasion, she had to stay in the same room as a young competitor and her Border Collie, Sprint.

"I had a real affection for Sprint, and she'd always snuggle up close to me. I vowed that I would have one of her puppies if she ever had a litter—and she did! That's how I ended up with Quicksilver Ready To Dance, or Dancer for short.

"I love Border Collies. I like their energy and eagerness. I'm a very active, physical person, and I wanted a similar dog. Dancer is just that.

"I started training Dancer as soon as I got her home. One of the most important training lessons is Wait. Border Collies are always one move ahead and often anticipate what is coming next. The 'Wait' command stops them, so they learn a routine *with* you, rather than guessing what *should* come next.

"Spinning was one of the first moves. This is very simple to teach, and just involves holding a treat and luring the dog in a circle. Her reward is to have a game with a ball or a tuggie, which she loves.

"Dancer also loves the music. I haven't seen a Border Collie that doesn't like music. Right from the very start, we trained with music. Dancer is a tiny Border Collie (26 lbs.), and has a preference for fast music—hip-hop, rock 'n' roll, and foxtrots! I know if she doesn't like a particular piece of music,

as she'll carry her head low, and you instantly know she isn't enjoying it!

"If she enjoys something, she gives all her energy. She does the fastest weaves ever. We call them 'Weaves whoosh.' Once she did them so fast, she did a little spin at the end, then another one! I said, 'Wow! Dancer, that's good!'

"She often improvises. I may choreograph one thing, but she may do another. Often it is because it is more of a natural move for her, and flows better in the routine.

"Dancer was just 16 months old when she took the bronze bar in her Musical Freestyle Proficiency Test and passed. This is where you

Perfect harmony: Patie Ventre and Quicksilver Ready To Dance

compete against a Standard. For bronze, you have one-and-a-half minutes in which to perform five moves, choreographed in a routine. Three weeks later, we took the bronze in Heelwork to Music.

"I love the communication you develop with your dog in Freestyle. In the proficiency test, if you use too many verbal commands, you are failed, so you are forced to develop new ways of getting the dog to do what you want. Dancer has learnt that if I raise my hand in the air, she should go to my left heel, and so on.

"Border Collies like new challenges and get bored if they have to do something over and over again. With Freestyle, the routines are always developing and changing, which Dancer loves. The attention of a Border Collie is very acute. The intense concentration on their faces is a real joy to watch. The breed is also so animated. The Border Collie lends something very beautiful to Freestyle.

"The costumes are very important for the performances. I have several costumes, including a black suit which has silver sequin musical notes on it and white figures dancing across the chest, and down each leg of my trousers. Dancer has matching silver sequin ankle bands and a sparkly ruffle collar.

"Doing Freestyle has taught me an awful lot about dogs and their characters that I never knew before. Dancer and I look at each other and know what the other one's thinking. She laughs at me and plays jokes on me. We have developed a bond I never knew I was capable of making with a dog."

raid your wardrobe for something suitable to wear, put on your favorite CD track, choreograph some moves into a routine, and away you go!

Spinning

Turning around on the same spot is one of the simplest moves for your dog to learn. For most dogs the promise of a treat or game as reward is sufficient motivation.

- Get your Collie to stand in front of you. Show him a tug-toy and move it around in a left-hand circle. By following the movement of the toy, your Collie should rotate on the spot. As he does this, say "Twist."
- As soon as he finishes his spin, give him lots of praise and reward him with a cuddle, and a game with his toy.

- Repeat the move until you can dispense with the toy, and a guiding hand, along with a voice command, are the only cues. Over time, your Collie will learn to do this move with only a voice command.
- Once your dog has mastered the move, teach him to perform it in the opposite direction. Move the toy in a right-hand circle and use a different voice command, such as "Whirl."

THE SHOW WORLD

Every dog owner thinks they have the most beautiful dog (or dogs) in the world. Then to take your dog into a ring and have an experienced judge place him high in the class is enough to make you swell with pride. Equally, there is nothing more deflating than getting up

To succeed in the show ring you must have a dog that conforms as closely as possible to the Breed Standard.

at the crack of dawn, traveling hundreds of miles to attend a show, only to be eliminated from the ring in the early stages.

Beauty, as they say, is in the eyes of the beholder, and the show world can be a fickle place. Although every dog is judged against a Breed Standard, which describes the ideal example of the breed, its interpretation can

CHAMPIONS

In the U.K., a Border Collie becomes a Show Champion if he wins three Challenge Certificates. To become a full Champion, he must also pass a Working Test, where he should show sheep-herding ability.

In the U.S., where sheep farming is not so commonplace, far fewer Collies are used as flock dogs, and they are not required to exhibit working ability before becoming AKC Champions.

differ from judge to judge, and your dog's performance from day to day can also vary.

The dedicated show enthusiasts learn to take the rough with the smooth, to shrug their shoulders at the end of a disappointing day, to give their dog a cuddle, and return home, still having had a good day out. If you see each nonplacing as a personal failure, the show world is not for you.

If, however, you take up showing for the good of the breed, for the simple enjoyment of showing off your pride and joy, and for the opportunity of meeting like-minded people from all over the country, then you will never be disappointed.

Of course, the most important reason for showing of the three listed above is for the good of the breed. Having lots of competition in the ring is beneficial to the breed. It means that only the dogs that come the very closest to the ideal Border Collie, as laid out in the Breed

Standard, can win prizes, setting a high standard to beat. It also affects the future progeny of the breed, as it means the winners, who are sought after at stud, will pass on their genes to the next generation.

First Step

If you are interested in showing, the first step is to contact your breeder, who will be able to advise you on your dog's chances. If they are favorable, he or she will also be able to give you further advice about how to apply for a show, etc.

If your Border Collie is not show quality and you are thinking of buying a suitable puppy, you should, again, consult your breeder. It's also advisable to visit shows to see as many different Border Collies as possible; this will help you to establish exactly the type of look you prefer.

Remember, an entire litter of show-quality puppies is incredibly rare; you may get only one pup that has potential from a litter of eight, and maybe that pup will not turn out to make it in the ring. Be prepared to buy a pup with show potential, only for him never to realize his promise. As well as excellent breeding, luck definitely plays a part in producing show-quality pups, as our case history (page 86) illustrates.

Try to avoid picking a very young pup—try to delay your choice, if possible. The older the pup, the better the breeder will be able to determine the pup's quality.

Stand and Deliver

The Border Collie should stand four-square. Some handlers prefer to "stack" the dog, physically placing it in the correct position. Others prefer to walk the dog into the correct

TOP TIPS

Top breeder Carolyn Ward (page 86) has listed five top tips for someone just starting out on a show career:
1. Consult your breeder—he or she will be able to give you lots of advice.
2. Do your homework—go to shows to see what people should do in the ring.
3. Take your Collie to ring-training classes.
4. Enjoy it!
5. Enjoy your dog!

The dog must be posed to best advantage to show off his conformation.

Carolyn Ward's first love was the German Shepherd. As a keen Obedience enthusiast, however, she realized that the only way to get to the top-class levels of Competitive Obedience in the U.K. was with a Border Collie. After a successful Obedience career with her Collies, and with a young family to cope with, Carolyn could no longer commit the time necessary for daily training. Knowing how crucial it is for Border Collies to have a hobby to keep them occupied, Carolyn decided to start exhibiting them instead.

"The first time I went into the show ring, it was just dreadful," says Carolyn. "There is a real pressure to perform. You start off with high hopes but nerves can get the better of you. As the years go on, you get better.

"My first dog, Kris, was of no fixed abode, so to speak, but the best friend I have ever had. He didn't have a show history or a distinguished pedigree, and was really the wrong dog for the show ring. Most novices learn on their first show dog, and so rarely do particularly well with them.

"It takes about six months to see an improvement in the handler. You have to learn not to fidget in the ring, or your nerves pass down the lead to your dog. But showing is like going on stage—the more you do it, the more you get used to it. Saying that, after 17 years of showing, and having received top honors, there are still occasions where the nerves take over.

"The early days of showing are always the worst. I remember taking Kris into the ring, alongside experienced breeders. You get big names in every breed, and the Border Collie is no exception. I remember being in complete awe of them. Then it dawns on you that you *are* able to compete, and you think, 'Yes, I can do this!' Now, people tell me that *they* are in awe of *me*, which I think is very strange!

"I've bred seven Champions now, and I know my dogs love showing. Border Collies

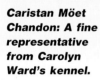

Caristan Möet Chandon: A fine representative from Carolyn Ward's kennel.

love being with you, and love pleasing you. If I leave a show dog at home, and take someone else out, the dog will create merry hell. They know where I'm going and want to come, too! Some of them will jump into the bath, as if to say, 'Where's our bath before we go out?'

"One of the funniest moments I've had was when I fell over in the ring. Kris continued running, went up to the judge, and did a perfect stand in front of him! That shows how much the dogs enjoy it—he did it without me. Another year, I was competing for the Reserve Challenge Certificate at Crufts. My dog, Caristan Lady in Red, had been asleep on the bench and I had to wake her up to get her in the ring. Just as she was being assessed, she gave a big yawn, as if getting that far at Crufts was just so dull!

"My first Show Champion was Caristan Captain. He was wonderful—a really special dog. He was from a litter of five pups where the dam would have nothing to do with them, so they had to be bottle-fed. You get very close to pups that you bottle-feed, especially when it is touch-and-go whether they live or die.

"I had bred the litter, as I wanted a bitch, but the litter was all boys. They all thrived and went off to homes, apart from one—Captain. I tried to find him a nice show home, but no one was interested. He soon wriggled his way into my heart, and I kept him. Luckily for me, he grew into a swan and became my first Show Champion, Sh. Ch. Caristan Captain.

"There's a real pride in showing a dog that you have bred yourself, especially when you have bred the parents or grandparents, too. I know some people have professional handlers, but I'd rather show my own dogs myself. It gives more of a sense of self-satisfaction."

position. A well-constructed Border Collie will stand in the show stance naturally, but sometimes the handler just needs to "tidy up" the feet, shifting them slightly to achieve a perfect stand.

The Collie should also show an alert expression. Some handlers "bait" their dogs to achieve this. Baiting involves the handler holding a treat to get the dog to look up and to appear keen. As soon as you are out of the ring, the dog should be given the treat as a reward.

Teaching the Stance

Teaching your Collie to stand in the show pose is very simple. Start from when your pup is still young. While he is standing up of his own accord, pet him, tickle his tummy, and use your command, such as "Stand-stay."

Spend just a few minutes every day doing this. As he gets used to standing still when you ask him, you can progress to trying to refine his stand, placing his legs four-square.

Practicing in front of a shop window allows the budding handler to see his reflection to assess what he and his dog look like to others.

Go to ring-training class, where your Collie will learn to stand with distractions all around him. Teaching an alert Border Collie to ignore chaos around him is never easy—they always want to know exactly what is happening around them—but perseverance with training is usually successful.

CHAPTER SIX

A SPECIAL BOND

Border Collies were bred to work with people, and this instinct is very strong in the breed. Although most Collies are now pet dogs, a significant number still work as sheepdogs. Their herding skills are also put to good use in search and rescue work, finding lost walkers and climbers, often in hazardous weather conditions.

The Collie's intelligence and love of serving his master makes him a successful assistance dog, helping the blind, the deaf, and the disabled to cope with everyday tasks.

SEARCH AND RESCUE

All over the world, search and rescue dogs work in a number of situations, finding lost and injured people. On television news reports you see them working with their handlers, investigating collapsed buildings caused by earthquakes or bomb explosions, alerting the authorities to the presence of survivors.

Most of the work, however, is done in more rural settings—in mountain ranges or extensive moors, where sudden and severe weather conditions can cause walkers to become lost, disoriented, and fighting for their lives.

Collies are a popular breed for this kind of work. Not only are they surefooted and agile, with considerable stamina, but they also have the right instincts for search and rescue. Bred to work in nasty weather conditions over difficult terrain when searching for lost sheep, they are preprogrammed for this sort of endeavor.

Search and rescue dog handlers are mountain rescue volunteers who give their time willingly. They never know when they will be called upon to drop everything, grab their dog and rucksack, and join a search. Usually, the weather conditions are poor, but the long hours spent searching often produce a happy ending that makes all the effort and exhaustion worthwhile. In some geographical areas, however, there are few happy endings, as our case history illustrates.

MOUNTAIN RANGERS

Jan Millar, from Glasgow, Scotland, is a keen mountaineer. It seemed natural to her to combine her love of mountains and her love of dogs, and so she volunteered for search and rescue work.

"My first mountain search dog was Rangitoto, a Husky-Alsatian type cross," says Jan. "After 18 months of training, in November 1988 Rangitoto achieved search and rescue dog status. Our first job together was in December 1988.

"I had been called out at 8 P.M. to go down to Lockerbie, which is about two hours' drive south of Glasgow. At that time it wasn't clear what had happened, and the information I received was that a light aircraft had crashed. It turned out to be, of course, the terrible Lockerbie air disaster. For the next 20 hours we searched and located people spread over a vast area of countryside and in the town itself.

"Because it was Rangi's first call-out, she was a little confused, as the rules of the training had changed. Usually, she would get a reward for finding articles belonging to a human, but because there were items scattered all over, and our priority was to find humans, I had to keep encouraging her to continue searching even when she had found an article. Rangi soon understood that we were ignoring the articles, and rapidly picked up what was required of her. Working with two other dog teams, during the night, we found the bodies of 24 people, some still strapped in their aircraft seats. It was an horrendous, surreal experience, which the dogs coped with magnificently.

"I retired Rangitoto in October 1996 and I now have two Border Collies—a pup called Buidhe and a four-year-old trained mountain search dog called Corrach.

"Training a search dog is all about encouraging the dog's natural instinct to hunt. The Border Collie is an intelligent animal which thrives on being challenged. You can harness the dog's natural ability by training him to search out human scent. The trick to a successful partnership with a Border Collie is to be able to direct the dog to cover the optimum area of mountainside using wind direction and natural features. It goes without saying that it takes the human element of

Jan Millar with Search and Rescue dog Corrach.

the partnership longer to learn how to search an area than it does for the canine half of the team!

"Search dogs are trained to ignore non-human scents on the mountainside, for example, deer carcasses, etc. At the start, however, you want to encourage your dog's natural curiosity. If your dog finds a person or article, he is rewarded. If he indicates on a nonhuman scent, you would ignore the indication and not praise the dog.

"Training takes an average of 18 months to two years. The dogs should be enthusiastic and eager to learn. After teaching the usual commands of Sit, Down, etc., the trainee search dog must learn to bark on command. It is also vitally important that the dogs get used to ignoring sheep, as they will be stock-tested by a shepherd on an annual basis. A firm 'No' when the dogs show interest, and regularly taking them near flocks, gets them familiar to seeing sheep, and should stop their natural instinct for eyeing the animals.

"The Border Collie is ideal for search work. These dogs need to use their intelligence for constructive action, to focus on something, and search and rescue work is ideal for them, as the training is continuous. Official training is one weekend every month, but I also train my dogs for about three hours a week. I vary the training in order to keep them alert, continually learning new scenarios. For example, on a walk, I'll throw a sock into a bush for the dogs to find, or place an old jumper halfway up a tree, just so they continue to develop their search skills.

"I have helped to rescue people in difficulties on many occasions when, as a mountain rescue team member, I have gone to their known position. However, when using my dog in a search scenario, I have yet to locate

Corrach working on a mountainside.

someone who is still alive. A lot of our more semirural searches are suicide cases.

"It is upsetting when you find a suicide victim, but there's always the hope that, one day, you will find someone alive and that you will make a difference in some way.

"I sometimes wonder why I continue to do search and rescue work when it can be so sad. I think it's a combination of enjoying training my pet Border Collie to be a search dog, and the challenge of moving in high mountains. I'm a teacher by profession, so it's nice to see the results of our training together, and see the enjoyment the dogs get out of it. Search and rescue work is all about working as a team; you have to send the dog to the right places. You could direct the dog to the left of a boulder, and there could be someone to the right of it. If the wind direction isn't favorable, that person could be missed, so I have to be very thorough about where I send the dog. The other reason why I do this kind of voluntary work is that I still have the hope that one day I'll make a difference and save someone's life."

SNIFFER DOGS

The Border Collie's natural search abilities are also put to good use as sniffer dogs, searching for explosives (for the army and police), for the causes of fire (for arson detectives), and for drugs (for customs officers).

EXPLOSIVE EMPLOYEES

Maggie Peacock has trained her own Border Collies for explosive detection work. Maggie is a former dog handler for the Army, and her husband worked as a bomb disposal officer, so they were able to combine their specialized knowledge.

"I saw a police demonstration search once," says Maggie, "and I thought 'I can do this.' So I did! At the time I had German Shepherds, who were extremely motivated in search work, but I had always wanted a merle Border Collie.

"I remember, years ago, seeing a red merle Collie standing by his owner outside an Obedience ring. The owner was talking to someone, but the dog spent about 20 minutes just collecting discarded cigarette ends and throwing them at his owner's feet to get her attention. It went on and on and on, and I remember thinking, 'Now, that is really compulsive.'

"My mother was a German Shepherd fanatic, though, so I had to wait until I left home before I could get a merle Collie. My first was a bitch called Breeze. She has as good a nose as my previous German Shepherds— Border Collies have been bred to search for lost sheep, after all!

"Like a German Shepherd, a Border Collie starts becoming reliable at about two-and-a-half years old, but the Collie's working life tends to be longer. A German Shepherd generally starts losing interest at about eight years of age, and is ready to retire, but a Collie usually remains eager. Breeze is now 12, and is still able to do a good night's work.

"Dogs are always using their noses, looking for food or a bitch. They are naturally curious, and always on the make! It's easy to harness this search instinct and put it to another use.

"I start 'training' from a very young age. I get the puppy interested in playing with a wide variety of toys and then progress to hiding the toys and getting the puppy to find

Sassy searches an industrial site for explosives.

them. The reward for searching is the toy. I will hide the toy in a variety of places—outdoors or indoors—and then start to introduce the smell of explosives to the toys. The toys don't actually contain any explosives, just the vapor. The toys continue to be hidden and the dog is rewarded with ten minutes of play with the toy when he finds it.

"My Collies are taught not to touch the toy, but to give a signal when they find it. Obviously, this is for their safety and mine—you don't want them playing with any explosives they find on a real search! The signal is taught by me holding their toy, and waiting for them to take one step back and give a bark. Collies often do this naturally if you have something that they want. If the dog rushes forward to me to get the toy, I will nudge him back a step to encourage the right response. He shouldn't be given the toy until he gives the right signal.

"Eventually, the dogs are introduced to a harness, which has no use whatsoever, apart from to signal to the dog that he must search—it is like his work uniform! When the harness is off, he should stop searching.

"At the moment I have four dogs—Breeze, Ryda (Breeze's son), Speck (Breeze's grandson), and Sassy (Breeze's great-great-granddaughter). We have searched all kinds of places, for all kinds of customers. We have searched for the government (though I can't give any details about this job as it was confidential work), and we have also searched TV studios, to ensure the place is clear before important guests appear.

"In our 13 years, we have never found any hidden explosives, but the dogs have found a lot more! They are taught to search only for explosives, but they seem to find anything that is a scent anomaly. They don't give the same signal as if they have found explosives, but they

A "find" is indicated by the dog taking a step back and barking.

become a little agitated and focus on a particular area. This way, they have found guns and gun oils. Once, when we were searching the Café Royal in London during the time of the Gulf War, the dogs found some silver that had been hidden in a wall panel. It had been stolen and stashed away, and never recovered by the culprit, who may have left their job, or moved on.

"If the dogs don't find something, and I know the room is clear of explosives, I will often go in at the end and hide one of their toys, then send them in again. This keeps them motivated—if they always searched, but never found anything, they would soon lose interest.

"Although my dogs are great workers, they are all show quality (with the exception of Breeze, who has excellent conformation but is mismarked). The boys have their stud-book number, and they have all qualified for Crufts in their time. It's important that the Border Collie breed doesn't lose its working ability, and my dogs prove that they can have looks as well as brains!"

DOGS FOR THE DISABLED

The kind of tasks that Dogs for the Disabled can be trained to do are remarkably varied, and very much depend on the owner's individual needs. They can be taught to switch lights on and off, fetch a cordless telephone or remote control, open and close cupboards and doors, help the owner undress, remove laundry from the washing machine, press elevator buttons, and so much more!

All training is based on play, and is made a fun, enjoyable experience for the dog. For example, a fun game of tug with a rope toy is only one step away from the dog tugging on a rope attached to a door handle in order to pull it open. And retrieving a handbag from the other side of the room is just an extension of a game of fetch. To the dog, it is all a game. To the disabled owner, however, it often means they can be independent.

Needless to say, the relationship between the recipient and the Dog for the Disabled becomes incredibly close. Not only are the dogs of great practical help, fetching things, picking up dropped items, opening doors, and so on, but they also become close companions, offering emotional support and love—something the devoted Border Collie excels at!

MAGICAL MEG

Ann Hendry from Caversham, Berkshire, suffered severe spinal damage following a riding accident. Ann has always been an admirer of Border Collies and has had them as pets, so she was particularly pleased when her Dog for the Disabled, Meg, turned out to be a Collie, too.

"Meg was a part-trained Working Sheepdog that was donated by a member of the public," explains Ann. "As far as I'm concerned, Collies are top in the brains department. Any breed from a working background has to be a plus, doesn't it?

Ann Hendry with Jade, her pet Border Collie.

Meg is certainly very keen. "I have to wear what is called a 'Boston brace,' which is a rigid plastic jacket so that I can't move my back. I also have a leg caliper. This means that if something falls on the floor, it has to stay there. Now, of course, Meg can fetch it for me. In fact, if something is within my reach, such as the phone, she gets annoyed if I don't allow her to hand it to me. She looks at me as if to say, 'Hmmm! That's my job!'

"I have such a lot of nerve damage in my spine that I can sometimes fall down—my brain can't tell my legs what to do. Meg has fetched help for me several times. She has been taught to 'speak' on command—where she'll bark until help comes. I have also told her to 'go to Lena,' my neighbor. She will let herself out of the house, go to Lena, and gently knock on the door. Then she listens. If no one comes, she shoulders the door, trying to nudge it open. If still no one comes, she goes nuts, as if to yell, 'Open this door, now!'

"Once, I fell between two parked cars while taking the dogs out. I just couldn't move, and because I couldn't be seen, there was a real possibility that someone would get in the car, slam it into reverse, and squidge me without realizing.

"I managed to get Meg free, and told her to go for help. It was one of those streets, though, where no one paid any attention to a barking dog, so I told Meg to go home. She ran the few hundred yards home—round a few corners—and tried to fetch help.

"It was a cold, frosty night, and while Meg was seeking help, my pet Collie, Jade, lay on top of me to keep me warm. Meg kept running back to me to check I was okay and to give me a lick, before running back to try again. In the end, she alerted the neighbors and led them to me. She was so pleased with herself! Her tail didn't stop wagging the whole time.

"I live on my own, and I have a carer come and visit in the morning and in the evening. Meg is a great carer. She does everything I need. She can even pull my socks and trousers off. If only she could cook, I wouldn't need anyone else at all!

"Meg is also my best friend. She accompanies me on all my hospital visits, where everyone makes a huge fuss of her. When you are a disabled person, people can be embarrassed to approach you sometimes, but all that goes when you get a Dog for the Disabled.

Meg, a fully trained Dog for the Disabled, has changed Ann's life.

Suddenly, everyone hones in on you wherever you are, just to make friends with the dog!

"Meg has impeccable manners, and expects everyone else to have them, too. For example, she has learnt to take my prescription in to the chemist's, give it to the pharmacist, and then go back outside to wait with me, while it is being dispensed. Then she'll go back in when it is ready, take the bag, and bring it to me (I never allow her to do this if the medication is in a breakable glass bottle). Letting Meg do this for me is much easier than negotiating doors and steps, etc. However, Meg will not let go of the prescription until the person behind the counter says 'Thank you.' If I need to pay in a shop, Meg will reach up to the counter with my purse in her mouth and, again, won't give it up until she hears 'Thank you.' She always insists on politeness!

"Meggie is the best thing to happen to me since I became disabled. A person can pick something up for you, but by the ninth or tenth time they get a bit fed up. Never with Meg. She takes me for who I am, not what I am. Meg has given me so much of my life back."

GUIDE DOGS

There are a fair number of Border Collies trained as guide dogs, but they are not used as extensively as the ubiquitous Retriever breeds. The problem isn't training the Collie for guide dog work, it is matching them to a suitable recipient.

The Border Collie is such an energetic breed that it needs an equally energetic owner— someone who walks at a fairly fast pace and who has a suitably busy lifestyle to satisfy the Collie's need to be kept active and occupied.

Often, Border Collies are crossed with Golden Retrievers, producing a calmer, more relaxed dog that is less sensitive to noise and generally works at a slightly slower pace, thereby suiting more potential guide dog candidates.

GUIDING LIGHT

Tony Kularachi's problems with her eyesight started some 20 years ago. An experienced Collie owner, Tony competed in Obedience and in the show ring. It seemed a natural step to train her own guide dog after she had lost her sight.

"After my sight loss, I did not immediately apply for a guide dog, but taught my own dogs to fulfill my needs," says Tony. "It was not until 1994 that (due to limited access for dogs in shops and public places) I found it necessary to register my Collie dog, Whizz, with the Guide Dog Association. Sadly, a couple of years after his registration, Whizz had to retire due to ill health.

"I then agreed to have one of the official guide dogs instead of finding my own pup and socializing and training him myself. This was only on condition that the guide dog would be a Border Collie.

"Within a few months, I had a phone call to say that Murphy, a blue merle Border Collie, was available. I was told that he had many allergies which caused him to have a loose tummy and he could be traffic shy if he was frightened, but I decided to embark on the training process with him.

"I will not pretend that the training period was a happy time. This is because I have a tendency to get frustrated, and all I felt Murphy was doing at that point was just avoiding obstacles on paths and roadways. One of my frustrations was that guide dogs are not taught to find room numbers in strange buildings or to find shopping in a supermarket. As my other dogs had done these things for me, I could not see why, at nearly two years old, Murphy couldn't.

"Murphy had also been kenneled, which meant that, typical of Border Collies, he was climbing the wall and going stir-crazy. During the evenings at home, Murphy would spend hours and hours chasing shadows and chasing his tail round and round. During the day, when we were out and about, Murphy was fine while we were moving, but as soon as we stopped, he would start digging or would launch himself at someone for a cuddle.

"My friends and I agreed that he was loony, but we finished the training period nevertheless. Now Murphy and I were by ourselves, and I made up my mind that I was going to try to teach Murphy the things my other dogs had done—shopping, for example.

I enjoy being independent, and I was not prepared to spend the rest of my life walking into a supermarket and asking for an assistant to find my shopping for me.

"To distract Murphy from chasing shadows and his own tail, we got the 'shopping game' under way in the evenings at home. The game starts with teaching the dog to 'Hold,' 'Retrieve,' and 'Find.' All three are then combined to make a game of hide-and-seek, except the dog is finding egg boxes and washing powder cartons—all manner of things instead of pet toys. Once the dog is finding the article and bringing it back to me, he

Tony Kularachi and Murphy: A partnership that has grown and developed.

is then taught to leave the article where it is and to take me to it. All the teaching I do is on a reward system—in Murphy's case it is a liver mixture that he cannot resist.

"Once I have all the shopping I need, I say to Murphy 'All done.' However, he won't take me to the checkout until I have said, 'Find the sweets then.' He then takes me to the dog-food aisle and I have to put a small bag of dog biscuits in the basket. Only then will he take me to the checkout!

"When Murphy can't find something, he stands still and I can feel his confusion—it is almost as if he is metaphorically scratching his head, saying, 'I don't know.' This is where 'Find help' comes in useful, another of Murphy's games. Murphy has been taught to go to a police officer, traffic warden, or shop assistant.

"Since last September, Murphy and I have had to commute every day on the train. Murphy has a clock inside him, and he believes that his train should always run on time. Anyone who travels daily by train knows that this does not always happen!

"If the train is not dead on time, Murphy starts getting fidgety, sitting up and lying down. This goes on for about five minutes. Then Murphy starts talking. It starts with a gentle 'Bo-ow' and gradually goes up three pitches. Each time, he sounds more fed up, and it is as if he is saying, 'My train is late; why isn't it here?'

"It's at this point that Murphy generally gets a reaction from one of my fellow commuters who will stroke him and explain to him that they are just as fed up, and that the train will be along shortly. When the commuter stops speaking to him, Murphy lies down with an audible thump and a 'humphhh.' It is almost as if he is saying 'Flipping trains!'

"I couldn't be without a Collie—they are so intelligent, almost like little people. My guide dogs have been my eyes. All I see is a dense fog, no shadows, nothing. If a dog doesn't take me out, or find my keys, or do scores of other things for me, I'm stumped. With Murphy, we're a bit like a married couple—he can be the biggest pest sometimes, but I just couldn't do without him."

THERAPY DOGS

Every owner knows how therapeutic dogs can be. There's nothing better to lift the spirits than to stroke a contented dog, and enjoy a good cuddle together. It can reduce stress and feelings of loneliness, and increase one's sense of well-being.

People in hospitals, hospices, or residential homes usually do not have access to a pet, and for animal lovers, this can leave a huge void. Therapy dog programs fill that void.

The programs rely on volunteers sparing a couple of hours of their time on a regular basis to take their dogs on visits.

The participating dogs must be well behaved and well socialized, and should enjoy meeting lots of new people. The dogs are assessed thoroughly to ensure they are "bomb-proof" and utterly trustworthy before they are registered and allowed to meet their adoring public.

Life in many establishments can be a little routine, and having a visit from a therapy dog can alleviate the boredom. It helps to introduce a new topic of conversation to the residents, and also provides them with the opportunity to chat with the dogs' owners and enjoy some human, as well as canine, company.

THREE'S COMPANY

As red-and-white, blue merle, and black-and-white Border Collies, therapy dogs Ana, Jack, and Rosie always bring a bit of color to people's lives.

"I started visiting with Ana, my red-and-white Collie, in March 1992, and she is now 11," explains owner Rosemary Shrimpton. "I had heard about therapy dog work, and wondered what it entailed. I found out more, and we were assessed to see if she had the right temperament. A therapy dog needs to be confident and friendly with everyone, and should not be shy, nervous, or withdrawn. Ana was trained in Agility and Obedience, so I knew she was well behaved, and she certainly has the right temperament.

"Once we passed the test and were registered, we started visiting a residential home for the elderly. Many of the residents were former dog owners and missed having pets. I thought that having a doggie visitor would cheer them up—which it did. They really came to life when they saw Ana. Some of the residents had lost their dogs or had to rehome them, and they were thrilled to bits to have contact with a dog again.

"About 12 months after I started visiting, I decided to breed from Ana, and the home was buzzing with people talking about the news— guessing how many puppies she'd have, what they would look like, etc. When the pups were born, I took in photos and it gave the residents a new topic of conversation. They had a genuine interest in Ana and her puppies.

"The owner of the stud dog I had used had been a patient at a nearby hospice, and

Ana's visits have brought color and interest to the elderly residents.

this time, Jack, my blue merle, and Rosie, my black-and-white, were also registered therapy dogs. They loved visiting as much as Ana did. Everyone appreciated our visits, and the dogs really brightened their day.

"We also started visiting warden-controlled sheltered accommodation, and the dogs soon worked out their own itinerary of whom they would visit and when.

"For the people we visit, seeing the dogs is the highlight of their week. Most people love dogs. You only have to walk down the street with a dog and people stop you and make a fuss of him. Dogs draw people together, whatever age they are. And my Border Collies love people—the fuss, the cuddles, the strokes, and the biscuits! They know when it's visiting day, and can't get out to the car quickly enough.

"I'd recommend the therapy dog program to everyone. It doesn't have to tie you down for hours of visiting. You only need an hour or two each week or each fortnight—whatever you can spare. To start with, half an hour is enough, as it enables the dog, you, and the residents to get used to it.

unfortunately, she passed away. She had requested that, instead of flowers being given for the funeral, that donations should be sent to the hospice. Having seen the effect of taking Ana to the old people's home, I thought it would be nice to visit the hospice, too.

"The hospice had a wider age range, from about 30 to 65, and had a great atmosphere. By

"You get to see such a change in the people you visit. Sometimes they can be so quiet and withdrawn, but when the dogs arrive, you see the sparkle in their eyes. It's also good for dog owners because it enables you to do something for the community and to share your dogs with people who really appreciate them."

CHAPTER SEVEN

SEEKING PERFECTION

The Border Collie is a very distinctive breed, which is why it is usually easy to tell when a crossbreed has a Collie parent. What makes it so easy to identify a Border Collie? Is it the alert character? The unmistakable Collie face? The lithe, yet solid-looking body?

It is no one single thing, but rather a whole list of details and characteristics unique to the breed that, when put together, create the Border Collie that is known and loved all across the world.

THE WORKING DOG

In the dog world, it is important to describe the ideal Border Collie, to have a written record of every point from the nose to the tail, so that all judges work from the same guidelines and judge each dog against an immutable picture of Border Collie perfection. This written blueprint is known as a Breed Standard.

The Border Collie Breed Standard emphasises that it is a working breed. If this ability is to be safeguarded, it is important that only the very best dogs (that is, those that come closest to the ideal portrayed in the Standard) are bred from. This ensures that the Collie's uniqueness is passed on to other generations.

BREED STANDARDS

This is a summary of the key points in the KC and AKC Standards, detailing the importance of the breed's characteristics to its working ability.

General Appearance

As well as giving the impression of endurance, the Border Collie should be athletic and agile. Tough and hardy, he should also be well balanced and graceful.

Characteristics

The KC Standard describes a "tenacious, hard-working sheep dog, of great tractability." The AKC Standard describes the Border Collie

The Border Collie is first and foremost a working breed, and it is vital that this heritage be safeguarded. Photo: David Dalton.

as the "world's premier shepherding dog." This is a working dog through and through, and his shepherding skills should come above any aesthetic considerations such as coat markings.

Temperament

The Border Collie should be keen and eager, alert, and intelligent.

Head and Skull

The skull should be fairly broad, and the occiput (the point at the top rear of the skull) should not be pronounced. The stop (the indentation between the two eyes) should be distinct. The Border Collie needs a broad skull to accommodate a large brain.

The nose color is very much dependent on coat color. Black-and-white dogs should have black noses, brown or chocolate dogs should have brown noses, and blue dogs should have slate noses.

The nostrils should be well developed so the dog can get sufficient air into his lungs while working strenuously.

Eyes

The Collie expression should be alert, intelligent, keen, and full of interest. This is a dog that always looks ready for work.

To ensure the Collie has good scope of vision while he is working, his oval eyes should be set well apart. Since they are set on a broad skull, the dog's span of vision is considerable.

Eyes should be brown, except in merles, where blue is permissible.

Ears

Like the eyes, the ears should be set well apart. The Border Collie should be sensitive to all sounds around him, whether it is his handler's commands, a stray lamb bleating, or the sound of a potential predator. To ensure his ears pick up as many sounds as possible, his erect or semierect ears should be set well apart, and should be sensitive and mobile.

Mouth

The teeth and jaws need to be strong. He should have a complete scissor bite (upper teeth closely overlapping lower teeth). In the past, sheepdogs had to survive on a reasonably coarse diet (scraps and raw meat), and needed strong teeth to be able to eat the food.

Neck

The Collie "working" position sees the dog with his neck low and outstretched, concentrating on his flock. He should have a strong, muscular neck of good length. It should be slightly arched, and should broaden to the shoulders.

Sheep were not always kept in short pasture. In longer grass, a Collie had to stretch his neck to full height to look for sheep, so a good reach of neck was crucial.

Forequarters

The forelegs should be parallel when viewed from the front. When viewed from the side, a slight slope in the pasterns (the area between the dog's "wrist" and his toes) should be visible. This conformation provides a "shock absorber" system. He needs strong bones to withstand grueling work, but they should not be heavy, as his speed and agility should not be compromised.

The skull is broad, and the ears are set wide apart.

Body

The Collie should have an athletic body designed for work. His ribs should be well sprung, this allowing for maximum lung capacity when herding, his chest should be deep (again necessary for heart and lung room), and his loins (the area below the ribs and above the pelvis) should be deep and muscular.

The body should be slightly longer than it is tall. This shape allows the most effortless, energy-efficient movement and is seen in other Collie breeds (such as the Bearded Collie). It also enables the dog to turn quickly. An overly long body would lose strength along the spine, but the Collie's length ensures the dog maintains power, mobility, and flexibility.

Hindquarters

The hindquarters have been compared to an engine room—the dog's source of power. Again,

The body is slightly longer than its height, and should be athletic in appearance.

The forelegs are straight and strong.

the mixture of hardiness and gracefulness is important. The hindquarters should be broad and muscular, as the Collie needs a powerful drive when working.

The thighs should be long and muscular, the stifles should be well turned, and the hocks should be strong and well let down. Again, this ensures a shock-absorber effect.

When viewed from behind, the back legs should be parallel; the AKC Standard permits slight cow hocks.

Feet
Because he should be able to work in different environments and conditions, the Collie needs strong "working boots"—that is, oval, compact feet with strong, deep pads; arched toes that are close together to ensure the dog remains sure-footed; and nails that are short and strong.

Tail
A tail can be compared to a rudder, and is especially important for enabling dogs to keep their balance when making fast turns (an essential quality in herding). The low-set tail should be long (the bone reaching to the hock), and may have a small curl at the end. It is held low while the dog is working, but may be held higher if the dog is excited. It should never be gay, which means carried over the back.

As with all dogs, the tail is an important means of communication. An experienced shepherd will be able to "read" his dog via the tail, noticing if the dog is confident around the sheep, or is angry, or subdued, or experiencing some other emotion.

Gait/Movement
Movement should be effortless and energy efficient, covering as much ground with the minimum number of paces possible. Although his gait should appear tireless, the dog should be capable of considerable speed and stealth.

Coat

There are two types of coat: moderately long, and smooth. In both varieties, the top coat should be dense, and the undercoat should be soft, dense, and weather resistant.

A mane (longer hair around the chest and neck) is permissible.

Color

A variety of colors and markings is permissible, though white should never predominate. This is because a white dog will not be easily noticed in a flock by the sheep or by the farmer.

Size

According to the KC, the ideal height for dogs is 53 cm (21 in.); slightly less for bitches. The AKC states a recommended height of 19–22 in. (48.2–55.9 cm) for dogs and 18–21 in. (45.7–53.3 cm) for bitches.

TYPES OF BREEDING

If you have a purebred registered Collie, and you can't make any sense of your dog's pedigree, examine the two following pedigrees on pages 107–108. Once you've compared your dog's pedigree with these examples, you should have a clearer idea of what breeding went into producing your special Collie.

The pedigrees illustrate linebreeding and outcrossing, two types of breeding that describe the degree of closeness between the dogs that are mated. With the right expertise, each one can be used successfully to create Champions, though each has its strengths and weaknesses.

Tri-color.

Blue merle.

Red and white.

Red merle.

Black and white.

Blue and white.

Linebreeding

Linebreeding involves mating dogs that are not so closely related, but that nevertheless share the same family. It is used by breeders to cement their type, and because the same family of dogs generally share the same characteristics, the results rarely come as a surprise.

Sh. Ch. Bekkis Genesis is linebred on Sh. Ch. Reakasso Ryan. It is a grandfather × granddaughter mating. Breeder Alison Hornsby always admired Sh. Ch. Mizanne The Witch (for type, conformation, and movement), so decided to double up on this line.

Sh. Ch. Bekkis Genesis proved a great success, exceling in construction, movement, and, most importantly, a superb temperament.

Linebreeding: **Sh. Ch. Bekkis Genesis.**

Parents	Grandparents	Great-Grandparents	Great-Great-Grandparents
Sh. Ch. Reakasso Ryan	Sh. Ch. Whenway Rhys of Mizanne	Sh. Ch. Asoka Navajho of Firelynx	Shep 73359
			Asoka Cloud 85227
		Wisp from Whenway	Sup. Int. Ch. Wiston Bill 51654
			Langloch Jenny 102007
	Sh. Ch. Mizanne The Lady Lucinda	Sh. Ch. Kathmick Griff	Langloch Glen 81784
			Jess 97842
		Sh. Ch. Mizanne The Witch	Asoka Apache of Firelynx
			Cass of Mizanne
Bekkis Charisma	Wizaland Newz Sensation	AUST. & NZ. Ch. Clan-Abby Casanova Too	AUST. & NZ. Ch. Maghera Casanova
			NZ Ch. Evening Sky of Clan-Abby
		NZ & AUST. Sh. Ch. Francesca of Clan-Abby	Clan-Abby Lorna's Brae
			AUST. & NZ. Ch. Rullion Joy
	Viber Ryan's Daughter at Bekkis	Sh. Ch. Reakasso Ryan	Sh. Ch. Whenway Rhys of Mizanne
			Sh. Ch. Mizanne The Lady Lucinda
		Sh. Ch. Viber Lovers Tiff	Sh. Ch. Cluff of Mobella
			Sh. Ch. Sacul Highland Mist from Corinlea

Outcrossing

Outcrossing is when two unrelated dogs are mated. The results of the mating are less predictable, but it is a useful form of breeding when you want to introduce new genes to your line. It is often used after a period of extensive inbreeding and linebreeding. Once the new gene pool has been introduced, linebreeding can be used to "fix" the type. As inbreeding and linebreeding can, on occasion, reduce fertility and overexaggerate some features, outcrossing can sometimes increase fertility and reduce exaggeration.

The pedigree of Sh. Ch. Reakasso Rock Symphony for Passim spans more than 25 years. Note that the dogs with numbers after their names are registered with the International Sheepdog Society only, as they were around before the Kennel Club recognized the Border Collie.

Outcross breeding: Sh. Ch. Reakasso Rock Symphony, owned by Sue Ader.

Parents	Grandparents	Great-Grandparents	Great-Great-Grandparents
Sh. Ch. Reakasso Ryan	Sh. Ch. Whenway Rhys of Mizanne	Sh. Ch. Asoka Navajho of Firelynx	Shep 73359
			Asoka Cloud 85227
		Wisp from Whenway	Int. Sup. Ch. Bill 51654
			Langloch Jenny 102007
	Sh. Ch. Mizanne The Lady Lucinda	Sh. Ch. Kathmick Griff	Langloch Glen 81784
			Jess 97842
		Sh. Ch. Mizanne The Witch	Asoka Apache of Firelynx
			Cass of Mizanne
Passim Crystal Spray	Wizaland Newz Speculation at Mobella	AUST & NZ Sh. Ch. Clan-Abby Casanova Too	AUST. & NZ. Ch. Maghera Casanova
			NZ. Ch. Evening Sky of Clan-Abby
		NZ & AUST. Sh. Ch. Francesca of Clan-Abby	Clan-Abby Lorna's Brae
			AUST. & NZ. Ch. Rullion Joy
	Passim ABI at Patlyns	Passims Dynamite	Toss 128262
			Jill at Passim
		Passims Wispa	Woodland Mirk at Passim
			Passims Rosie Lee

PUPPY TO CHAMPION

Sh. Ch. Tonkory Palmerston at Fayken

Owned by Ross and Vicki Green, and bred by Judith Gregory, "Taz" has an impressive record: to date—at the age of three—he has seven CCs and ten Reserve CCs.

12 weeks of age.

14 weeks of age.

21 months.

**Two-and-a-half years old and a Show Champion.
Photo: Lynn Graham.**

Detecting a Champion, when faced with a litter of eight or so tiny pups, is beyond the ability of most people. To the untrained eye, the pups probably all look the same, but an accomplished breeder and exhibitor has considerable experience to draw from, and is more likely to pick a winner than a "layperson."

However, even with experience, it can all go awry—a promising pup could grow to be too "leggy" or "snipy," or simply not enjoy being in the ring. Equally, an eight-week-old no-hoper could turn into a showstopper. All puppies progress differently, but to give you an idea of how your pup may develop, see how the Border Collie above grew to become a Champion.

CHAPTER EIGHT

HEALTH CARE

**Trevor Turner
BVetMed, MRCVS**

The Border Collie is a highly intelligent dog with an inborn instinct to work. Looks have always come second to working ability, which in turn depends upon stamina, agility, and intelligence, qualities that have also contributed to his success in the show ring.

Being medium-sized dogs, around 21 inches (53 cm) to the shoulder, they have few "breed-prone" problems, as do the majority of dogs that have been bred basically for work. In some strains, however, nervous conditions (including epilepsy) have become a problem, and certain joint conditions (including hip dysplasia) are not unknown. The major disease predisposition relates to eye problems, and these, together with the other specific breed health problems, will be discussed separately.

PREVENTIVE CARE

Preventive care obviously covers vaccination and parasite control, but other factors are important.

The Border Collie is a highly active working machine. Thus a correctly balanced diet and plentiful, regular exercise are essential.

Exercise

Exercise is paramount and is probably the most important area of preventive care. Swift movement is part of the heritage of the Border

The Border Collie is not a dog for the sedentary owner.

Collie, and, given the opportunity, puppies will run till they drop. However, hip dysplasia and other bone problems (see page 127) do occur in the breed, so exercise must be controlled, particularly while your Collie is immature (until approximately 12–18 months of age).

Because of their intelligence, Collie puppies are eager to learn, so part of the exercise program should involve training, which you can start as soon as you get the puppy home. You should also enroll at a basic obedience training class when your pup is 4–6 months of age, depending on your local club and your puppy's rate of development.

Having trained successive generations of puppies over the years, I find that intelligent, responsive pups, such as Border Collies, will find a quarter of an hour's basic lead-training just as exhausting as an hour's walk (which they shouldn't be subjected to at this age). Half an hour at a good training class and the puppy will be exhausted and sleep for several hours. Broadly speaking, the more active the puppy, the more sleep and rest he needs, so a half-hour training session and four hours of sleep makes a good combination.

Once over a year old, exercise must be adequate for the dog's needs; otherwise boredom will supervene. These are not dogs for sedentary owners. However, the nervous energy expended by the dog in Obedience or Agility work relieves the owner of miles of foot slogging—so do not think that Obedience work for the Border Collie is just for puppy training.

Your inability to stimulate, extend, and exercise the young, healthy adult Border Collie can produce major behavioral problems, which are clearly not the dog's fault. This has to be accepted as one of the responsibilities of owning this very active breed.

VACCINATION

Vaccination, by definition, involves subjecting the body to a suspension of micro-organisms altered so that they stimulate immunity. Vaccination against infectious tracheitis (kennel cough), for example, is administered by instilling a few drops up the nose.

Inoculation involves introducing the agent into the tissues of the body. Today, this is usually

First immunity is acquired from the dam.

by injection. For our purposes, vaccination and inoculation are synonymous.

Passive Immunity

The puppy acquires his first immunity from the dam while in the womb. The necessary antibodies cross the placenta and enter the puppy's bloodstream. After birth, immunity is topped up (boosted) by the same antibodies in the bitch's milk.

This is passive immunity, and once the puppy is weaned, it soon fades. This is when the puppy should receive his vaccinations. These will stimulate the puppy to build up his own active immunity. This does not last indefinitely and boosting will be required.

The question of regular boosting is a contentious issue in some dog circles today. In my view, boosting is important; without it, we could rapidly return to the situation when diseases such as distemper and parvovirus were rife.

Primary vaccination should be carried out as soon as the passively acquired immunity from the bitch has declined sufficiently to allow the puppy to respond to the vaccine. Canine vaccines are available today that will stimulate the puppy to develop a solid, active immunity even if some maternal antibodies are still circulating. The full vaccination program can be completed by 10–12 weeks of age.

Immunity Gap

These vaccines attempt to overcome the so-called "immunity gap." This has always been a

The intelligent Border Collie needs to socialize with other puppies.

problem with canine vaccination. For the vaccine to stimulate the puppy's immunity, circulating antibodies against any of the diseases contained in the vaccine must have fallen sufficiently. Vaccination takes time to stimulate the puppy's immune system, and during this period the puppy could be vulnerable to infection. In the past, this often meant isolation from possible sources of infection (that is, other dogs, and places frequented by other dogs) until an immunity had developed.

This happens at the same time as the puppy, particularly a breed like the highly intelligent Border Collie, needs to meet as many new experiences as possible in order to mature into a well-integrated family dog, accepting strangers and other animals with equanimity.

Some Border Collies, like some children, are inherently shy. These cases particularly need early socialization. Thus the new generation of vaccines is a real step forward. I am convinced that many difficult dogs in the past were the result of isolation until four months of age or beyond while the inoculation took effect.

Once you have acquired your puppy, call your local veterinarian and discuss vaccinations, appointments policy, price, and so forth, and at the same time find out whether the practice organizes puppy classes. Obviously, the sooner you can get your new Border Collie puppy to meet other dogs, the better. Early socialization with any of the working or pastoral breeds can do nothing but good. Puppies grow particularly fast, and Border Collies, with their well-developed brains, need early, controlled socialization.

Booster Vaccinations

Boosters have recently become a matter of concern for both veterinarians and dog owners. Polyvalent (multivalent) vaccines give protection against several diseases. They are very popular, but concern has been voiced that these cause adverse reactions, and their very need has been questioned.

However, veterinarians are urged to follow the manufacturers' instructions with any drugs, including vaccines. In order to obtain a product license, vaccine manufacturers have to submit evidence regarding the safety and efficacy of their product. With a vaccine, this will include

the duration of immunity. Because of cost and other factors, this is usually looked at over 12 months. Hence when a product license is issued, provided there is no evidence of reaction on boosting immunity, a recommendation will be included for this to be done after one year.

Revaccination is currently under review by manufacturers. Some are suggesting that, with certain diseases (for example, distemper and hepatitis), annual boosting may not be strictly necessary. My personal view is that the risk of reaction is so slight, compared with the threat of disease in the unprotected dog, that I would rather be accused of overvaccination than have to experience a dog with any of the very serious diseases for which we routinely vaccinate today. In 40 years of busy canine practice, I have never had to treat a dog with a serious vaccine reaction.

If you have concerns, discuss the matter carefully with your veterinarian at the time of primary vaccination. He or she will be able to discuss the risks and benefits with respect to your particular animal and in relation to disease prevalence in your locality.

Measuring Immunity

Blood tests are available for both puppies and adult dogs that will indicate the animal's level of immunity for any of the diseases against which we normally vaccinate. These will give a guide to the necessity for revaccination. However, be forewarned: it is likely that the cost of testing for each disease will be as much as a combined booster against all the diseases. Money apart, it is also arguable whether this blood testing is in

Kennel cough is highly infectious and will spread quickly through a group of resident dogs.

the dog's best interest. Taking a blood sample from most puppies, and for a fair number of adult Border Collies, is a stressful procedure—considerably more stressful than a booster vaccination, which can cover anything up to six diseases with one quick and simple injection.

Core and Noncore Vaccines

Acknowledging the drawbacks associated with some vaccines, there has been a move in the United States to divide vaccination into two groups: core vaccines and noncore vaccines.

Core vaccines protect against diseases that are serious, fatal, or difficult to treat. In the U.K., this includes distemper, parvovirus, and adenovirus (hepatitis). In the U.S., rabies is also included in this category of necessary protection. As a result of the change in the quarantine laws in Great

Britain, rabies vaccine is now freely available from veterinarians and may well become a core vaccine in the not-too-distant future.

Noncore vaccines include Bordetella, Leptospirosis, Coronavirus, and Borrelia (Lyme Disease). This latter vaccine, used widely in North America, is known to cause reactions in a number of dogs. Lyme Disease is a tick-borne disease that is of considerable concern in North America. It does occur to a lesser extent in the UK. In Britain, there is not currently a licensed vaccine available against Lyme Disease.

Kennel Cough

Depending on the disease, some vaccines do not endow long-lasting immunity. The intranasal Bordetella bronchiseptica vaccine against infectious tracheitis/bronchitis (kennel cough)

lasts only approximately eight months. The same can be said of natural immunity after a bout of the condition. If not challenged by contact with the disease, immunity is likely to drop to dangerous levels in about six months. Thus, if you regularly board your dog, attend training or Obedience classes, shows, and so on, revaccination against Bordetella (kennel cough) every six months is money well spent.

Kennel cough is described as having low mortality and high morbidity: it does not often prove fatal, but the dog will usually cough for several weeks. Even when apparently recovered, he can still act as a carrier. Such a situation could be disruptive to any training program involving your new Border Collie.

To complicate matters further, kennel cough is not caused by Bordetella alone. Parainfluenza virus is another contributor; indeed in North America this virus is considered to be the major cause, whereas in Britain and the rest of Europe, Bordetella (a bacterium), is considered to be the most important agent, with parainfluenza playing a secondary role. In addition, adenovirus and distemper virus also play a part. All of these are incorporated into the usual polyvalent (multivalent) vaccines that are routinely administered.

Recently, a new intranasal kennel cough vaccine has been introduced that contains not only Bordetella but also a parainfluenza component as well. This vaccine will reinforce immunity conferred by the conventional parainfluenza component administered as part of the normal inoculation.

Leptospira

Leptospira vaccines are also usually included in the primary vaccination course. These cover two serious bacterial diseases caused by Leptospira bacterial organisms, *L. canicola* and *L. icterohaemorrhagiae*. These are killed vaccines and provide protection for only about 12 months. The modified live virus vaccines (for example, distemper or parvovirus) give a much longer period of protection, but this varies with the individual and the disease.

Canine Distemper

Today, canine distemper is relatively rare in most parts of Britain and the highly populated parts of the United States, solely because of vaccination. Signs (symptoms) include fever, diarrhea, coughing, and discharges from the nose and eyes. Sometimes the pads will harden, a sign of the so-called "Hardpad" variant. Further signs— fits, chorea (twitching of groups of muscles), and paralysis—can be seen in a high proportion of infected dogs. As mentioned, distemper virus can be involved in the kennel cough syndrome.

Hepatitis

Also known as adenovirus disease, hepatitis can show signs ranging from sudden death with a peracute infection to mild cases in which the patient is just a bit "off-color." Most cases present with a fever, enlargement of all the lymph nodes (glands), and a swollen liver. During recovery, "blue eye" can occur. This is because of edema (swelling) of the clear cornea in front of the eye, and the dog may look blind.

Initially very worrying, this usually resolves quickly without impairing sight.

Adenovirus can also be one of the components in the kennel cough syndrome.

Rabies

Rabies is present on all continents except Australasia and Antarctica. Several countries, of which the U.K. is one, are free of the disease, usually because of geographical barriers. The virus does not survive long outside the body. The vectors of the disease are wildlife, particularly foxes or stray dogs. Transmission is mainly by biting and the signs are caused by disruption of the central nervous system by the virus. It is an extremely serious disease communicable to humans (zoonotic).

Vaccination using an inactivated (killed) vaccine is mandatory in many countries, including the United States. With the relaxation of quarantine regulations in Britain, rabies vaccines are now available from veterinarians and are mandatory if British travelers wish to visit Europe and return with their dogs under the PETS travel plan or to reside in EC countries.

Infectious Tracheitis/Bronchitis

Infectious tracheitis/bronchitis can be serious, particularly in very young and very old dogs. It causes a persistent cough, and as explained, in the United Kingdom the bacterial organism *Bordetella bronchiseptica* is considered the primary causal agent; in the United States, parainfluenza virus is usually considered the main cause.

A parainfluenza component is incorporated in many multivalent vaccines, and Bordetellosis prevention is achieved with separate intranasal vaccination. There is also a combined parainfluenza/Bordetella vaccine that has recently become available.

Lyme Disease

Lyme Disease is a tick-borne bacterial disease causing acute, often recurrent, polyarthritis in both dogs and humans. Fever, cardiac, kidney, and neurological problems can also occur in some cases. A vaccine is available in the United States.

PARASITE CONTROL

Parasite control is very important with your Border Collie. These are working, outdoor dogs intended for flock duties. It is not surprising that parasites can be a problem without preventive care.

Parasite control involves both **ectoparasites** (for example, lice, fleas, and ticks) and **endoparasites**, which include roundworms, tapeworms, and hookworms, together with heartworm, which is important in southern Europe and North America.

Ectoparasites
Fleas

Fleas are the most common ectoparasite found on dogs. Some dogs will carry a very high flea burden apparently without problems, whereas others will develop a flea allergy dermatitis, sometimes as the result of only a very few flea bites. This is caused by the development of a hypersensitivity to the flea saliva, which is injected when the flea bites. This causes serious itching. Rather than developing an immunity to the flea bites, these unfortunate Border Collies tend to get worse as the season progresses and often have a practically hairless strip along the midline of the back. These animals require particularly vigilant flea control.

Fleas are not host specific. Dog and cat fleas can be found on dogs, cats, and humans. Hedgehog fleas can also be a problem in Border Collies in suburban or rural locations in Britain and northern Europe. In parts of North America, raccoons can be the main vector of fleas. Human fleas are very rare. All types of fleas can bite all species of animals, including us.

Life Cycle

Effective flea control involves knowing a little of the life cycle of the flea. Eggs and the larval (immature) form of the flea develop off the host. Development time depends upon both humidity and temperature. In warm environments, particularly with high humidity, the life cycle is completed in days rather than weeks. This is one of the reasons that fleas are such a problem in Britain in summertime and in the southern states of the United States all year round.

Fleas can survive in suitable environments for more than a year without feeding, which is why dogs and people can get bitten when entering properties left unoccupied for quite long periods of time.

Effective flea control involves adult fleas on the dog and the immature stages, which develop in the environment. Obviously, control of developing fleas in the yard is not practicable, particularly if continuously reinfested from visiting wildlife, such as hedgehogs or raccoons.

Fleas must have a meal of blood to complete their life cycle. They feed on the dog, then lay eggs, which develop in the environment. These may actually be laid on the dog and drop off, or the flea may hop off the dog to lay them.

Spot-on protection is an effective means of controlling fleas.

Flea Control

In the home, control should include thorough vacuuming to remove all the immature stages. The use of an environmental insecticide with prolonged action to kill any developing fleas must be considered, since few insecticides currently on the market will kill flea larvae.

Control of fleas on the dog can involve oral medication taken by the dog to prevent completion of the life cycle of the flea. The flea ingests the compound when it bites the dog for a blood meal. In addition, sprays, powders, or "spot-on" preparations can be used to kill any adult fleas present. Insecticidal baths effectively kill adult fleas on the dog but do not have any lasting effect. Therefore bathing must always be combined with other methods of flea control.

Some Border Collies are upset by the noise of sprays, be they pressurized or pump types. Powders tend to be messy, so modern spot-on preparations that give reasonable protection lasting up to two months (even if your dog is bathed between applications) are probably the most effective.

"Spot-ons" disperse a chemical throughout the invisible fat layer that covers the skin of a healthy dog—the chemical is not absorbed into the body. Very quickly (within 24 hours) the dog has total protection against fleas. On biting the dog, the flea's mouth parts have to penetrate through the fat layer to get to the blood, and it is in this way that the flea receives the parasiticide. This is an ideal preparation to use if your Border Collie happens to have a flea allergy dermatitis since you must then ensure that you use something to kill the adult fleas quickly. Some of the potent sprays with long residual action are also very effective if your dog will tolerate the noise.

Oral medication, preventing completion of the life cycle of the flea, is effective for long-term control but does not stop the mature fleas, which cause the problem when they bite the allergic dog for that essential blood meal in order to reproduce.

Lice

Lice are not as ubiquitous as fleas, but they can be a problem in Border Collies enjoying a rural outdoor lifestyle, particularly when they are in contact with farm stock. Unlike fleas, the whole life cycle occurs on the host, and the eggs (nits) are sticky and attach to individual hairs. Infestation with lice is invariably accompanied by intense pruritis (itching). Most flea preparations are effective, as is bathing with insecticidal shampoo.

Ticks

Ticks can be a problem in some areas, both in the U.K. and in North America. They are important since they can be the carriers of various diseases that can affect your Border Collie. Lyme Disease, Babesiosis, and Ehrlichiosis are examples.

There is a variety of insecticidal products available, and many of the flea and louse preparations are licensed for tick control. Some of the spot-on preparations in particular have prolonged activity even if the dog is bathed several times between applications.

Harvest Mites

Harvest mites are the immature forms (larvae) of a mite that lives in decaying organic matter. The tiny red larvae are just visible to the naked eye and are picked up by dogs exercised in fields and woodland locations, particularly with chalky soils. The feet and muzzle are most commonly affected.

The use of prolonged-action insecticidal preparations is recommended since reinfestation is likely, particularly if your Border Collie spends a lot of time in the locations described.

"Walking Dandruff"

"Walking dandruff" is an apt description! It is caused by a tiny, whitish, surface-living mite, which can just be seen by the naked eye.

Cheyletiellosis, to give it its official name, is not uncommon in farm-reared Border Collies. The pups will be particularly itchy, especially along the midline of the back, which, on examination, will show an increased amount of scurf or dandruff, some of which appears to move—the mites themselves! Treatment with any of the usual insecticidal preparations, baths, sprays, and so on is effective.

The mite lives only on the host, but older Borders can act as symptomless carriers. Care should be taken since the mite is zoonotic, that is, it will affect humans (particularly children) and causes intense itching.

Mange

Border Collies are popular pets today and as a result there is a ready market for puppies, some of which, regrettably, are less than adequately reared. In consequence, it is not uncommon to see Border Collie puppies with mange. This is a parasitic skin disease caused by microscopic mites. Two types usually infest dogs.

One, the **Demodectic** mite, lives in the hair follicles and causes a problem only in individuals whose immune system is incompetent for any reason. Demodectic mange (Demodex) does occur in Border Collies but is not seen as commonly as scabies or **Sarcoptic** mange, which is caused by a microscopic mite that burrows in the surface layers of the skin, and is extremely contagious and extremely itchy.

Although mites are fairly host specific, and most spread from dog to dog, foxes, raccoons, rabbits, and coyotes can also act as reservoirs. It is a highly contagious condition to humans, particularly children (causing scabies) and is fairly common with farm-bred puppies.

Diagnosis of mange depends on identification of the causal mite under a microscope. Effective treatments are available from your veterinarian.

Endoparasites

Worms are by far the most important endoparasite as far as your Border Collie is concerned. There are others, such as Coccidia and Giardia, which are tiny one-celled organisms that can occasionally cause diarrhea and lack of growth, particularly in poorly reared puppies.

Roundworms

Roundworms are the most common worms in the dog. *Toxocara canis,* the most common

It is essential to guard against roundworm in a family with small children.

Border Collie puppies with heavy worm infestations may have problems ranging from generalized poor growth to diarrhea and vomiting, to obstruction of the bowel and even death in the case of very heavy worm burdens.

Adult dogs can become infected by sniffing other dogs' feces, which is a normal behavior pattern in the dog.

Tapeworms

Tapeworms or cestodes are the other major class of worms found in the dog. They differ from roundworms in that they have an indirect life cycle, which means that spread is not directly from dog to dog but must involve an intermediate host. These vary according to the type of tapeworm, but the most common tapeworm in the dog (and cat), *Dipylidium caninum,* uses the flea as the intermediate host.

Dipylidium caninum can measure up to 20 inches (50 cm) and lives in the intestine. Many eggs are contained within mature segments, which look like grains of rice and break off from the end of the worm. These are passed in the dog's feces. The eggs are microscopic. Immature stages of the flea (larvae), which are free living, ingest the microscopic eggs, which mature as the flea develops. The mature flea is then swallowed by the dog and so the life cycle of the tapeworm is completed.

Effective tapeworm remedies are on sale in pet outlets and supermarkets without prescription, but, since effective control also involves rigorous flea control, it is worthwhile discussing this with your veterinarian.

roundworm, is a large, round white worm 7–15 cm (3–6 in.) long. The worm undergoes a complicated life cycle in the dog, and larvae (immature forms) can remain dormant in the tissues of adult dogs for long periods. In the bitch, under the influence of the hormones of pregnancy, these immature forms become activated. They cross the placenta and finally develop into adult worms in the small intestine of the puppy. There is a slight risk that humans, particularly children, can become infected with roundworms from dogs. Therefore, regular worming of your Border Collie, at least twice a year, is a wise precaution.

Another type of tapeworm that has importance in the Border Collie is *Echinococcus granulosus*. This is a very small tapeworm, only about 6 mm long (one-quarter of an inch). One intermediate host is the sheep and hence its importance in Border Collies. It is rare in the U.K. (although it does occur in parts of Wales) but is common in sheepdogs in North America. It is important because it can also affect humans.

Border Collies that are fed raw meat unfit for human consumption can also be infected with the *Taenia* species of tapeworm. This can also occur if they regularly catch and eat prey, since intermediate hosts include rabbits, as well as moose, deer, sheep, and goats.

Most tapeworm infections occur in adult dogs. Usually the first signs noted by most owners are little wriggling "rice grains" around the dog's anus. These are the mature segments containing eggs that have to be eaten by the intermediate host to complete the life cycle.

Effective tapeworm remedies cover all types of tapeworm and should be administered regularly to your Border Collie, particularly if he has a rural, outdoor lifestyle.

Heartworm

Heartworm, or *Diarofilaria Immitis,* is a major problem in many warmer parts of the world. It does occur in Great Britain but, to date, only in imported animals. Transmission is by bites from mosquitoes. Effective remedies are available.

Hookworms, Whipworms, and Lungworms

Hookworms, whipworms, and lungworms can also cause problems in certain areas. Your veterinarian will advise if any special remedies or precautions have to be taken in this respect.

EMERGENCY CARE/FIRST AID

Border Collies, no matter how well trained, are just as prone to accidents and emergency problems as any other dog. Emergencies come in all forms, from road traffic and other accidents, to bites and burns, to heat stroke, insect stings, and poisoning. Border Collies engaging in Obedience, in which the majority of the breed excel, can suffer torn nails during scaling exercises.

In addition, fits, convulsions, or seizures can be a problem in certain individuals, since epilepsy is not unknown in the breed.

First aid is the initial treatment given in an emergency. The purpose is to preserve life, reduce pain and discomfort, and minimize the risk of permanent disability or disfigurement. Irrespective of the emergency, there is much that can be done by simple first aid.

Priorities

- Keep calm and do not panic.
- If possible, get help. Contact your veterinarian, explain the situation, and obtain first-aid advice, if possible.
- If there is a possible internal injury, try to keep the dog as still as possible, placing him on his side on the ground. The head and neck can be gently pressed to the ground with your arm across the neck, if necessary holding uninjured limbs. This helps to keep the dog still while awaiting assistance.

- If your dog is in shock, it is important to keep him warm. Use a blanket if available or wrap him in a coat or even newspaper.
- If there are no spinal injuries, cradle him in your arms.
- If he cannot walk, gently carry him suspended in a blanket carried between two people holding the corners.
- If the injuries involve the back end, you may be able to move the dog by grasping him firmly around the chest and letting the hindquarters hang. In this way you are unlikely to cause further injuries. Many people try to move immobile dogs using boards, doors, and so forth as makeshift stretchers. The dog, if not actually unconscious, may be frightened with this unusual mode of transport and injure himself further by falling off!
- If at all possible, get someone to travel in the back of the car with the dog when you take him to the veterinarian.
- Drive carefully and observe the speed limits.

Shock

Shock is basically due to lack of fluid in the cells, tissues, or organs, or the body. It results in a serious fall in blood pressure. This can be caused by severe bleeding, heart failure, acute allergy, heat stroke, or something else. First signs include rapid breathing and increased heart rate. The mucous membranes (such as gums, lips, under the eyelids) look pale and the dog may appear depressed. His feet or ears may feel cold to the touch. Vomiting may occur.

Border Collie owners should have a knowledge of the principles of first aid.

Try to conserve heat. Cover with coats, blankets, or even newspapers. Keep as quiet as possible and seek immediate veterinary help, particularly if there is hemorrhaging, which should be controlled if at all possible.

THE A, B, AND C OF FIRST AID

A—AIRWAY
B—BREATHING
C—CARDIAC FUNCTION

AIRWAY: This always comes first in the A, B, C approach to first aid. If your Border Collie has injured his throat, perhaps playing with a stick, and is vomiting, collapsed, or choking, do your best to clear the airway. This allows the unobstructed passage of air (oxygen) to the lungs. **DO NOT PUT YOUR FINGERS IN THE MOUTH.** Your dog will be just as frightened as you are and, if fighting for his life, may well bite with panic.

Sometimes you can open the mouth using a blunt instrument between the teeth or by dropping a loop of material (such as a tie or even a piece of string) around the upper and lower fang teeth and gently pulling the mouth open. It may then be possible to remove the obstruction. Provided the dog cannot close his mouth on your hand, it may be possible to remove carefully any blood clots or vomit from the throat.

BREATHING: If your dog does not appear to be breathing, try gently pumping the chest with your hand, at the same time feeling behind the elbow to see if you can find a heartbeat (pulse). If not, cardiac massage can be tried (see below).

CARDIAC FUNCTION: With a hand on each side of the rib cage, just level with the elbows, with the legs pulled slightly forward, gently squeeze the ribs over the heart. Depending on your Border Collie's size, you may find it easier to use both hands. Squeeze approximately 15–20 times a minute, stopping every 10 or so to see if you can detect a heartbeat.

Emergencies
Bleeding
Torn nails are not uncommon in Border Collies. They are extremely painful and bleed profusely, as do cut pads. Improvise a tight bandage from any reasonably clean material. A polythene bag then bandaged over the paw, between the layers of bandage, will contain the blood. The main aim is to apply as much bandaging as possible

and then get the dog to the veterinarian without delay.

If you have had to bandage the limb very tightly, make sure that it is not left on for more than 15–20 minutes. If the site cannot be bandaged, try to control the bleeding by applying finger or hand pressure, preferably with a piece of clean dressing between your hand and the wound.

Burns and Scalds
Burns and scalds can happen very unexpectedly. Cool the burned area with cold water as quickly as possible. Use wet towels if extensive. Caustics (such as drain and oven cleaners) can burn. Try to dilute with plenty of cold water. If in the mouth, wash using cloths soaked in clean, cold water pressed between the jaws.

Eye Injuries
Eye injuries are not uncommon in the breed, because of foreign bodies or scratches (from cats' claws or bushes). Cover the eye with a pad soaked in cold water or, better still, saline solution (contact lens solution) and then seek veterinary help as soon as possible.

Heat Stroke
Border Collies are not particularly prone to heat stroke. It usually occurs as a result of being left in cars with too little ventilation in sultry weather. Remember, the car need not necessarily be in direct sunlight to kill your dog.

First signs are excessive panting with obvious distress; unconsciousness and coma quickly follow. Try to reduce body temperature by bathing in copious amounts of cold water, iced if possible, and then cover the still-wet animal in damp towels. Take him to the veterinarian as soon as possible. If driving there, make sure that as much air as possible is circulating over the dog. Evaporation will help to bring his temperature down.

Fits and Seizures

Fits caused by epilepsy and other causes can occur in some Border Collies, and these are always frightening for the onlooker. It is better not to touch the dog while he is in the fit so that he is not stimulated further. Left alone, injury is unlikely, particularly if any movable furniture (stools, occasional tables, and so on) are moved out of the way. A dark environment speeds recovery, so try to draw the curtains and turn off the lights. Once recovered, the dog will be dazed and unable to see or hear properly for a short time. Take care in handling him because he may be frightened and may not recognize you. As soon as practicable, take him to your veterinarian.

If the fit lasts for more than three or four minutes, contact your veterinarian for advice.

BREED-SPECIFIC PROBLEMS

Selected essentially for their working ability over centuries, it is hardly surprising that the Border Collie has rather fewer breed-specific problems than beset other breeds. However, there are a few diseases that seem to be overrepresented in the breed, and these fall broadly into three categories:

1. Eye problems
2. Joint disorders
3. Nervous diseases.

Genetics obviously play a part and in some countries, such as the U.K. and the United States, there are eradication plans in place for some problems. Contact your breed club and national kennel club for details. Nervous diseases, particularly epilepsy, are less common and there is, as yet, no officially approved control plan. However, dogs of any breed with even a suspicion of inherited problems should not be bred from.

Eye Problems

Basically, three eye problems affect the Border Collie:

- progressive retinal atrophy (PRA)
- collie eye anomaly (CEA)
- primary lens luxation

Mature onset cataract is also under investigation within the breed, but as yet no conclusions have been drawn as to its significance.

Progressive Retinal Atrophy (PRA)

The retina is the light-sensitive surface within the eye and can be likened to the film in a camera. Progressive Retinal Atrophy is the term used to describe a number of inherited retinal degenerations. In the Border Collie it is the central form of PRA that causes concern. This is also known as Retinal Pigment Epithelial Dystrophy (RPED).

It appears to be genetic in origin. There is a gradual loss of the central field of vision, but the dogs do maintain peripheral sight so that they do not go blind. Consequently, many owners do not realize there is any problem.

Under the joint BVA/KC plan in the U.K., veterinary ophthalmologists examine dogs' eyes for this and other possible inherent defects and certify accordingly. Other countries also run programs. Contact your breed club and kennel club for details.

Collie Eye Anomaly (CEA)

Collie Eye Anomaly does not cause blindness, although there is visual impairment. Again, it is detected as part of the routine screening program. Unlike CPRA, which, as its name suggests, is progressive, CEA is present from birth. A small proportion of affected animals may develop further complications such as retinal detachment and intraocular hemorrhage, but like CPRA, the condition often goes unnoticed by owners unless these complications occur.

Primary Lens Luxation

Primary Lens Luxation describes a condition in which the transparent lens situated within the eye, which serves to focus images on the light-sensitive retina, separates from its attachments and moves either forward or backward in the eye. If the lens moves forward, it is likely to interfere with the drainage of fluid from the eye and the extremely painful condition of glaucoma can develop. Although it can occur as the result of trauma, it does also occur in certain strains of Border Collies as a familial trait.

Unlike the preceding conditions, lens luxation can be treated very successfully. Provided the

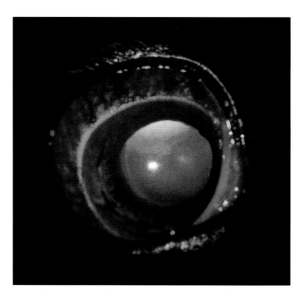

Swollen reddening of the eye, caused by glaucoma.

condition is diagnosed sufficiently early and the increased pressure caused by the glaucoma has not caused damage to the retina and optic nerve, veterinary ophthalmologists will routinely remove the lens and thus save at least some sight.

It is important to remember that if you have any concerns regarding the appearance of your Border Collie's eyes, you should seek advice from your veterinarian without delay. Time is of the essence, and if lens luxation has occurred, referral to a veterinary ophthalmologist can be sight saving.

Joint Problems

Although now a recognized breed for exhibition purposes, Border Collies have, for centuries, been bred for their working abilities. Sheep herding is arduous ground-covering work, and therefore, it is not surprising that joint problems should creep into the breed. These are basically two in number:

Hip Dysplasia

The term *dysplasia* means "abnormal growth." Hip dysplasia is a developmental condition that results in abnormal looseness or laxity of the hip joints. It is currently accepted as a multifactorial disease with heredity, nutrition, trauma, and exercise all influencing the outcome. The genetic component is caused by the interaction of many genes, and therefore it is called a *polygenic condition.*

On both sides of the Atlantic there are screening programs in place in an endeavor to reduce the amount of hip dysplasia within the breed. In the U.K., this is a joint British Veterinary Association/Kennel Club (BVA/KC) eradication program under which the dog is x-rayed in a standard position by your own veterinarian. X rays are then scored by a panel of specially trained veterinary experts. A maximum score of 53 is awarded to each hip so that the worst possible hips would score 106. Under this program, breed mean scores (BMS) are published with the advice that breeders wishing to reduce the risk of hip dysplasia should choose stock with scores well below the BMS. The number of Border Collies (Working Sheepdogs) scored under the scheme at 6.10.99 was 3,840; of those, scores ranged from 0 to 89, with a BMS of 14.

If contemplating buying a Border Collie puppy, it is advisable to ask if the parents have been scored for hip dysplasia and to ascertain the individual scores. The puppy will not have been scored, as dogs are not eligible until they are more than a year old, although the Orthopaedic Federation of America (OFA) scores them at an earlier age.

Osteochondritis Dessicans (OCD)

Osteochondritis dessicans is a condition that results in fissures in the growing cartilage in the joints. This can, on occasion, result in a loose flap of cartilage in the joint (joint mouse), particularly in the shoulder and the elbow. This occurs between four to ten months of age, when the dog may show sudden signs of pain and lameness.

Although there is a familial predisposition in certain strains, like hip dysplasia it is multi-factorial; also like hip dysplasia, the condition can be exacerbated by overactivity on the part of

Exercise must be limited during the vulnerable growing period.

the puppy during the rapid growing phase from four months onward.

Treatment involving medication and/or surgery is very effective, but even in individuals with a familial predisposition to the condition, the severity can be reduced by ensuring that the pup does not overexercise until cartilage growth is completed, at approximately 12–18 months of age. Otherwise, there is the possibility of the early onset of arthritis in the affected limb.

Nervous Problems

Border Collies would not be able to do their job so well if they had not evolved as being "situationally aware." Temperamentally, they are highly tuned and thus can sometimes become highly strung!

With good care and management, your Border Collie will enjoy a happy, healthy life.

Epilepsy, Seizures, or Fits

Epilepsy, seizures, or fits can occur from time to time in all such dogs although, let it be said, other breeds of working dog are far more prone than are Border Collies. Nevertheless, epilepsy does occur in the breed. When fits occur in otherwise healthy animals, this is known as *Idiopathic Epilepsy.*

Modern drug therapy controls the condition so that the majority of patients can lead perfectly normal lives. Indeed, some epileptic Border Collies excel in Obedience competitions and Trials. However, treatment is a long-term commitment, although some dogs can be gradually weaned from their anticonvulsants. In entire bitches, fits are often associated with

the reproductive cycle, and therefore, it is worthwhile considering neutering as an option.

If you have a Border Collie that has one fit, it does not mean you have an epileptic dog. However, when purchasing a puppy, it is advisable to inquire about the temperament in general terms and to ask if there have been any nervous problems or fits in the line.

HEALTH SUMMARY

Although, as with any breed, emergencies can occur, Border Collies are remarkably healthy dogs. Preventive care and early training will help to ensure many years of active companionship from this wonderful dog, whose breed motto should perhaps be "we are younger, longer."